Madrid, Spain

2025 to 2026

Fun Experiences, Must do's and Hidden Gems

JourneyJoy Journeys

All rights reserved.

No part of this publication may be reproduced, distributed, or transmitted in any form or by any means, including photocopying, recording, or other electronic or mechanical methods, without the prior written permission of the publisher, except in the case of brief quotations embodied in critical reviews and certain other noncommercial uses permitted by copyright law.

Copyright © JourneyJoy Journeys, 2025.

Madrid is a dynamic story that fascinates and pulls you into its rhythm. The city offers something beautiful for you regardless of your interests: history enthusiasts, foodies, or simply folks who like losing themselves in vibrantly colored streets. And this guide? Whatever kind of visitor you are, this is here to enable you to sink straight into the core of the Spanish city. Madrid will make you feel as if you have stumbled into a postcard full of culture, excitement, and maybe even too much sangria; but is that really possible? There are a lot of hidden gems of plazas and tapas eateries there.

You should definitely visit the well-known attractions, though let's not stop there; Madrid's essence is found in the small things, say like; the elderly man chatting on a bench, the aroma of freshly baked churros filling the air, or the impromptu shouts for a street artist who just performed well, it all adds to the charm. Pack light; you'll need room for mementos; embrace the vibrant Madrileño culture; get ready to experience a city that wants to be felt rather than just seen. This guide will provide your compass, insider information, and maybe simply a reason for a second jamón dish. We guarantee you that Madrid is worth every second.

CONTENTS

A DAY IN THE LIFE: MADRID EDITION 7

MADRID: A PLACE WITH STORIES AROUND EVERY CORNER 10

PLANNING YOUR VISIT 12
An Overview of This Guide and How to Use It 12
Weather and Year-Round Packing Advice 14
Madrid's Transportation Options 17

EXPLORING MADRID'S ICONIC LANDMARKS 21
Delving into Madrid's Rich History and Culture 34
Family-Friendly Activities 51

CULINARY EXPERIENCES, NIGHTLIFE AND ENTERTAINMENT 60
Traditional Tapas Tour 60
Must-Visit Restaurants and Must-Eats 68
Flamenco Shows 80
Trendy Rooftop Bars with Stunning Views 91

HIDDEN GEMS AND OFF-THE-BEATEN-PATH — 99

SHOPPING AND SOUVENIRS — 124

SIMPLE SAMPLE ITINERARIES — 134
A 7-day Family-Focused Itinerary: Activities for All Ages — 134
A 7-Day First-Timer's Madrid Itinerary — 140
A 7-Day Romantic Madrid Itinerary — 147

PRACTICAL TRAVEL TIPS — 153
Budget Breakdowns for Madrid on the Move — 153
Madrid Packing Checklist — 157
Safety Tips and Local Etiquette — 161
Basic Spanish Phrases — 166
Emergency Contacts and Information — 170
Essential Touring Apps and Resources — 175

FINAL WORDS — 181

A DAY IN THE LIFE: MADRID EDITION

Here is a question for both young and old: How can one enjoy Madrid without getting overwhelmed by the amount of tapas, sangria, and passionate flamenco music? Trick question! But of course, you accept it all. The streets of this city are buzzing with history, gastronomy, and a generous dose of madrileño mischief, and the days are long and the nights are longer. Let's experience a day in Madrid, including late-night churros and café con leche.

Madrid mornings are more leisurely rather than rushed. Start at a local café with a buttery croissant and a café con leche. Imagine having a cup of coffee and watching the individuals in Plaza Mayor. Have you seen the bird that is continually too curious for its own good? You can stroll to El Retiro Park from there. Renting a rowboat or masquerading like a Spanish aristocrat while wandering by fountains and sculptures are other good ideas. Feeling cultural? Visit the Prado Museum, where Goya and Velázquez are waiting to be appreciated. Just take your time; Madrid mornings are supposed to be appreciated, not rushed.

As afternoons say hi, your stomach may be growling louder than the street entertainers at this point. Order the famed fried fish at a traditional tapas bar like Casa Revuelta. In Spain, it's never too early to combine it with a vermouth. Think about having a siesta after lunch. If you try taking a nap and things aren't working out, just let it slide and visit the Royal Palace, where you will be in awe of its majesty and silently marvel at how someone could have maintained such a big space in pristine condition.

With Madrid's evenings, the city gets bustling with bustle as the sun sets. Explore the streets of La Latina or Malasaña, where cafés and bars abound on cobblestone streets. Savor additional tapas, like jamón ibérico or patatas bravas, while laughing with new companions. The night isn't complete without a trip to Chocolatería San Ginés for churros and chocolate. Pro tip: dip, don't dunk; otherwise, you'll appear like a tourist (but honestly, who cares?). It's great either way.

Every day feels like a celebration in Madrid, and you're always invited. You can be a morning stroller or a night owl, either way, this lively city has something special waiting for you. Just remember: in Madrid, the finest plans are frequently no plans at all (but be sure to make those plans).

MADRID: A PLACE WITH STORIES AROUND EVERY CORNER

Madrid is a symphony of culture, history, and dynamic energy that captivates you at every step. Its cobblestone streets are like turning the pages of an old storybook, but with vivid plazas, eye-catching architecture, and a cast of folks that make you feel as if you've joined a movie set. Here, the present comes to life with every flamenco dance and joyous laugh that explodes from tapas cafés, while the past resonates through Gothic buildings.

But what is that one thing that makes Madrid so enchanted? It's the ease with which opposites merge together. While your evening might involve exciting flamenco performances and a table loaded high with croquetas, jamón, and just one more bottle of Rioja, your morning might find you touring the majesty of the Royal Palace, steeped in history. This mix is reflected by the Madrileños, the locals, who effortlessly achieve a balance between their love of tradition and an indisputable passion for life. Not to mention the hidden riches Madrid has to offer those who are willing to delve a little deeper: secret gardens, eccentric cafés that resemble a comfortable hug, and tranquil places where time seems to stop still. Madrid demands that you feel it, not just see it. This city never fails to leave an impact, it can be via the dreamy light provided by the golden sunset, the sound of clinking glasses and laughing, or the rhythmic strumming of a guitar radiating from a welcome bar. The surprises and those few moments of astonishment will keep you coming, even if you only come for the major sights.

PLANNING YOUR VISIT

An Overview of This Guide and How to Use It

This guide is meant to make your holiday memorable, make it simpler for you to navigate around the city, and help you find activities that interest you. Iconic sights, must-try eateries, hidden gems and regional secrets are all included to improve your trip. To make sure there is something for everyone, the guide also includes ideas for family-friendly activities and seasonal highlights.

Each place mentioned in the guide is coupled with a QR code to further expedite things. You do not need to overly rely on these QR codes, they are simply for your convenience when you decide to make reservations and bookings. To get the location of a particular place on Google Maps, simply use your smartphone to scan the code. In addition to directions, this feature gives a plethora of additional information, such as photographs, reviews, and even options to schedule bookings, tickets, or excursions. Everything you need is only a scan away, so there's no need to look for particulars. The structure of the guide is meant to allow you both inspiration and independence. We've also included useful advice to guarantee a seamless journey, such as how to utilize the city's first-rate public transportation system and where to seek economical alternatives without compromising quality. So make use of it to research, learn about, and fully experience all that makes this city distinct.

Weather and Year-Round Packing Advice

Madrid's climate is as diverse as the city itself, with particular attractions to be explored in every season. By being informed of what to expect, you can organize your vacation properly and make sure you're ready for all the city's skies may throw at you.

- **Spring: March through May**

Madrid's springtime is beautiful, with agreeable temperatures between 10°C and 20°C (50°F and 68°F). Blooming flowers and outdoor patios filled with visitors bring the city to life. Your best choice is to wear light layers, as in lighter shirts or blouses throughout the day and a comfortable jacket or cardigan for cold mornings and evenings. Because spring showers could arrive as a surprise, remember to take a small umbrella.

- **Summer: June through August**

The hot, dry summers in Madrid regularly hit highs of 35°C (95°F). To keep cool in the heat, carry light, breathable garments, like linen or cotton. Given how powerful the Spanish sun can get, it is necessary to pack a wide-brimmed hat, sunglasses, and sunscreen. For exploring, comfortable sandals or walking shoes are necessary, and to be hydrated, don't forget to pack a reusable water bottle. If you want to stay out late, you won't need much more than a light layer, as nights are warm.

- **Fall: September through November**

With the temperatures slowly lowering from the summer highs, autumn is yet another great season to visit. It's the excellent time of year for walking trips and park visits, with normal temperatures that range from 10°C to 25°C (50°F to 77°F). Layering is important; a lightweight scarf or sweater is appropriate for cool evenings, and a waterproof jacket will be handy in the case of periodic rain.

- **Winter: December through February**

Madrid experiences cool but never freezing winters, with daily highs of 6°C to 12°C (43°F to 54°F). Wearing a scarf, gloves, and a large coat will keep you warm, more so if you're out wandering in the nighttime. And since snow rarely falls in Madrid owing to its dry atmosphere, boots that are comfortable and durable are a smart alternative, as mornings can turn cold. Because heating in certain older buildings could vary, carry suitable layers for internal spaces.

- **All-Year Essentials**

There are some items that should always be in your luggage, regardless of when you visit. Madrid is a city that is best explored on foot; hence, good walking shoes are needed. Your basics, such as a portable phone charger, a reusable water bottle, and your travel paperwork, are best carried in a lightweight backpack or bag.

Madrid's Transportation Options

Madrid's functional, diversified, and well-connected transportation infrastructure makes going about the city an adventure in and of itself. Regardless of your level of expertise, the city offers a range of activities to meet your time, interests, and budget.

Madrid is the favorite alternative for both inhabitants and visitors thanks to its metro system, which is among the largest and most functional in Europe. It connects the city's key attractions, residential neighborhoods, and even the airport with 12 lines that run throughout the city and beyond. During peak hours, trains run every two to five minutes, assuring quick wait times, and to make the most of a metro:

- Purchase a Multi Card, a reusable travel card available at Metro stations.
- For unlimited travel over one to seven days, buy a tourist pass; this is the best choice for traveling.

- Get familiar with Metro maps and note significant hubs such as Sol and Atocha stations.

The bus system in Madrid acts as a complement to the Metro, providing service to regions that the Metro does not. Since some bus lines (referred to as "búhos" or night owls) operate around the clock, buses are particularly beneficial for short excursions or late-night commuting. Bus travel provides a scenic alternative to the underground Metro, enabling you to take in Madrid's landscapes via broad windows. The tickets are fairly priced and can be purchased directly from the driver (exact change essential) or paid for using the Multi Card. For the convenience of planning, bus terminals give complete timetables and route maps.

The Cercanías trains provide a speedy and friendly method to explore outside the city core. These trains, managed by Renfe, connect Madrid with adjacent towns, airports, and tourist spots such as Alcalá de Henares and El Escorial. They're a fantastic alternative for day trips or going to Madrid's major train terminals, Atocha and Chamartín.

Taxis in Madrid are available all throughout the city and are white with a red line. Fair pricing is assured by their metered nature. Finding a green light on the roof or heading to the right taxi stands are the two methods to hail one. You can also book journeys in advance for convenience by utilizing taxi applications like FreeNow. Taxis are a comfortable alternative for late nights or hauling big baggage, but they are more pricey than public transit. Uber, Bolt, and Cabify are also offered as modern replacements for regular taxis. These services are app-based and allow cashless payment and upfront pricing. They are especially handy for travelers who don't know Spanish or who would prefer to have customized door-to-door care.

With dedicated bike lanes and rental schemes like BiciMAD, the city's official e-bike sharing program, Madrid is becoming a more bike-friendly town. Biking along the Manzanares River or touring Madrid's parks, including Retiro or Casa de Campo, is a terrific experience when you hire a bike. Bicycles can be easily picked up and left off at BiciMAD stations situated throughout the city.

Transfers at the Madrid-Barajas Adolfo Suárez Airport are straightforward to travel to and from. The city center and the airport are instantly linked by Metro Line 8. An option is the Airport Express Bus, which travels around the clock and makes stops at significant areas like Atocha and Cibeles. There are also ride-sharing services and taxis that charge a predetermined fare for journeys from the airport to the center of Madrid.

When Taking Public Transit;

- For route planning and real-time updates, download the official Madrid Metro and EMT Madrid apps.
- For buses or smaller stations that may not accept cards, keep replacement money on hand.
- Watch out for pickpockets, especially on crowded buses and Metro lines.

EXPLORING MADRID'S ICONIC LANDMARKS

Madrid is home to several famous attractions that combine beauty, culture, and history, and every one of them has a tale to tell:

- **Museo Nacional del Prado**

One of the greatest art museums in the world and a foundation of Madrid's cultural identity is the Museo Nacional del Prado that is situated at *Retiro*. The Prado is a haven for art enthusiasts, home to a vast collection of masterpieces from the 12th to the 19th centuries. It is a must-see for those interested in European art, as it features paintings by well-known artists such as Velázquez, Goya, and El Greco. Goya's ominous Black Paintings, El Greco's brilliant, spiritual compositions, and Velázquez's Las Meninas are some of its highlights. Hieronymus Bosch's The Garden of Earthly Delights and paintings by Rafael, Titian, and Rubens are among the other masterpieces. Goya's harsher paintings are on show, spanning numerous floors and even a basement, each giving a distinct story and perspective on the evolution of art. It is advisable to buy tickets online, which start at $15 per person, in order to optimize your visit. In addition to saving time, this gives a smoother admittance procedure, particularly during busy periods. The museum is open every day from 10 a.m., and the optimal times to visit without crowds are in the early morning or late afternoon.

Inside, a well-planned floor arrangement makes it easy to explore your favorite works of art or particular collections. Note that photography is not permitted, but this constraint adds to the immersive experience by enabling you to completely enjoy the displays' magnificence. Set aside a few hours to truly experience the Prado's attractions due to its large collection and quiet environment. For added convenience, there is a café on the site where guests can rest and refresh in between exploring this richness of creative inspiration.

- **Temple of Debod**

Situated at *C. de Ferraz, 1, Moncloa - Aravaca,* in the green parkland of Madrid's Parque del Oeste, the Temple of Debod is an intriguing monument that was transferred from Egypt to Spain. This ancient temple, which was initially erected in the second century BC near Aswan, was presented to Spain in 1968 as a thank-you gift for helping to protect Nubian monuments while the Aswan High Dam was being built.

With its complex hieroglyphics and old carvings, the temple's stone architecture is still authentic. While the surrounding nature provides a calm backdrop for meditation, visitors can explore the temple's interior and learn about its rich history. Although admittance is free, due to limited daily availability, tickets must be registered for, online in advance. Located in the city of Madrid, this unique opportunity to immerse oneself in ancient Egyptian culture is open daily from 10 a.m. to 7:30 p.m. (closed on Mondays). Beyond the historical value of the temple, its elevation on a little hill gives spectacular views over Madrid, making it one of the city's greatest spots to observe a beautiful sunset. In the evenings, the nearby park comes to life, creating a tranquil and lively environment as both locals and visitors take in the stunning landscape. The temple's façade is particularly gorgeous, and its majestic entryway is great for getting spectacular images. To avoid crowds and have enough time to absorb the beauty and quiet of this old gem, it is advisable to visit early or late in the day.

- **Santiago Bernabéu Stadium**

Both football lovers and curious travelers should make time to visit the Santiago Bernabéu Stadium, the home of the historic Real Madrid situated at *Av. de Concha Espina, 1, Chamartín*. This iconic stadium that can house an amazing 81,000 people, is steeped with passion and history and celebrates the triumphs of one of the most wealthy football clubs in the world. Starting at $37 per person, guests will enjoy an immersive stadium tour to see the field, VIP seats, and trophy room, stuffed with endless prizes. Interactive displays and videos that commemorate Real Madrid's incredible heritage and innovations; like the meticulous preservation of the stadium's grass, are also part of the experience. The Bernabéu is a genuine temple of football because of the amazing view from the pitch and the bustling atmosphere on game days.

Beyond the games, the Santiago Bernabéu tour shows the club's history with unique displays, including player souvenirs and the European Cups. Some areas do demand some walking, and the walkway is well-designed to guarantee you can see all the attractions. Following their visit to the stadium, guests can relax in adjacent cafés and bars, which are great for taking in the atmosphere before or after the game. A great range of items, suitable for gifts or souvenirs, are available in the official Real Madrid shop on-site. The Santiago Bernabéu Stadium is a celebration of grandeur, history, and the international phenomenon that is Real Madrid, with its state-of-the-art facilities, beautiful architecture, and historical relevance.

- **Catedral de Santa María la Real de la Almudena**

Adjacent to the Royal Palace at *C. de Bailén, 10, Centro*, the Catedral de Santa María la Real de la Almudena is a beautiful blend of Neo-Gothic, Baroque, and modern architecture. Its construction began in the late 18th century and was completed in 1993, making it relatively contemporary compared to many historic European cathedrals. Its bright interior and modern stained-glass windows form a dramatic contrast to its more traditional façade.

The Romanesque crypt, a calm space rich in history and finely designed, is accessible to guests and serves as a nice spot to reflect. A look into both past and current religious craftsmanship is afforded by the cathedral's chapels that enrich the experience with their intricate embellishments and bright artwork. The main cathedral is accessible to everyone, and entrance is by donation. The museum gives extra information about the cathedral's history and importance to Madrid for those who wish to explore further. Ascending to the dome, which affords breathtaking panoramic views of Madrid, including an exceptional vantage point of the Royal Palace, is one of the highlights of a visit to the cathedral. Two levels of view, including an open terrace where the city comes to life, are available with tickets for this experience. The rooftop terrace is particularly wonderful after sunset, when the surrounding buildings are lighted by the warm light. The cathedral's various roof designs are stunning, with each part presenting a unique piece of art. The cathedral is a renowned place that merges history, art, and spirituality. It's a site to pause, take in, and get a feel for Madrid's rich architectural and cultural past.

- **Royal Palace of Madrid: Palacio Real de Madrid**

Anyone visiting Madrid must tour the Royal Palace of Madrid (Palacio Real de Madrid), an architectural masterpiece tucked at *Centro*. With more than 135,000 square meters and an amazing 3,418 rooms, it is the greatest palace in Western Europe and among the largest in the world. One of the few royal palaces open to the general public, this lavish

18th-century house is used for big events and official occasions. While exploring rooms decorated with magnificent artwork, elegant furnishings, and precious relics, guests can immerse themselves in centuries of Spanish history. It is a real masterpiece of regal grandeur because of its outstanding architecture, which includes the excellent design of its interior rooms and its ridge-top position overlooking the city. Visitors should obtain tickets online in advance to prevent long waits, which may be especially challenging in Madrid's sunny environment. Tickets start at $16.

In order to thoroughly grasp the palace's large collection of gems and profound historical relevance, a tour normally lasts at least two hours. The enormous Banquet Hall, the beautiful Royal Chapel, and the spectacular Throne Room are among the highlights. Interesting insights into the history of the Spanish monarchy and the palace itself may be gleaned via audio guides or guided tours. In order to improve the experience, guests can also search for certain events like the Changing of the Guard ceremony. To wrap up this investigation of Madrid's royal history, it is highly encouraged to make a visit to the adjoining Almudena Cathedral, which is located immediately across from the palace.

- **Puerta del Sol**

Located in the middle of Madrid, the Puerta del Sol is a busy and renowned public plaza that acts as a social and cultural focus for both locals and visitors. It gives an immersive look at the bustling pulse of the city and is open twenty-four hours a day. Known as the "Sun's Gate," this lively area, which is home to numerous boutiques, cafés, and attractions, is a perfect place to start your tour of Madrid. The famous Kilometer Zero monument that commemorates the beginning of Spain's national road network, is situated there. The square's rich historical and cultural value is further boosted by noteworthy monuments such as the Mariblanca statue, the Bear and Strawberry Tree statue (El Oso y el Madroño), and the equestrian statue of King

Carlos III. Notable landmarks like the Royal Post Office (Real Casa de Correos), which is frequently the heart of New Year's Eve celebrations, and its iconic clock surround the area. Puerta del Sol is a terrific area for visiting, taking photographs, and soaking in Madrid's rich culture due to its vibrant and engaging environment. Indulge in gastronomic excursions, indulge in street entertainment, or explore neighborhood cafes and stores. With various bus and subway lines, it is also a transportation hub that is readily accessible from many regions of the city. There is also a direct metro connection to the airport. All visitors are treated to a spectacular experience as the region is converted into a festive paradise with shimmering Christmas lights and events during the holiday season. It is a must-see, but you should be careful of the crowds and probable pickpockets.

- **Plaza Mayor**

One of Madrid's most well known attractions is the Plaza Mayor, a gorgeous place steeped in beauty and history. This majestic plaza was initially erected in the 17th century by King Philip III and has served as the setting for many major ceremonies and gatherings. The plaza features nine remarkable arches that operate as its entrances, and it is bordered by finely built, uniformly formed buildings with their typical red façade. The majestic 1616 equestrian statue of Philip III that embodies the glory of Spain's Golden Age, is positioned in the core of the edifice. Being a pedestrian-only area, the plaza is the perfect place for enjoying a leisurely stroll and soaking in the lively surroundings.

The Plaza Mayor, flanked with modest cafés, traditional restaurants, and retail shops, gives a lovely combination of tastes, sights, and sounds. It's a hub of activity where artists, musicians, and street performers generate a cheerful attitude throughout day and night. With subtle lighting illuminating the arches, the ambiance transforms as evening creeps in, creating a mysterious sight. Visitors can savor traditional Spanish tapas, peruse local gift stores, and take in the site's timeless beauty.

- **El Retiro Park: Parque de El Retiro**

A wonderful sanctuary, El Retiro Park (Parque de El Retiro) delivers the perfect blend of outdoor enjoyment, cultural activities, and natural beauty. Encompassing more than 300 acres, this enormous park from the 19th century is a haven for leisure and pleasure. With its well-kept gardens, lush trees, and colorful flowers, the park offers a calm environment for jogging, yoga, walking, or resting in the center of nature. The renowned boating lake, where guests can rent rowboats and take in the wonderful views of the majestic monument to Alfonso XII that faces the water, is situated in the center. Every area of the park is a joy to explore, owing to its exquisite rose garden, tranquil fountains, and intriguing sculptures.

El Retiro also acts as a hub for pleasure and culture. Visitors could be in awe of historic structures like the Velázquez Palace and the Crystal Palace, a spectacular glass pavilion that regularly hosts art exhibitions. For those who are searching for peace and quiet, the lovely walks and shaded chairs offer the perfect area to relax and enjoy a picnic among the trees. Here, tourists, joggers, families, and dog walkers mingle, creating a crowded and tranquil location. Visitors can enjoy a snack or drink while soaking in the scene at the small outdoor cafés located throughout the region. Open every day from 6 AM to midnight, El Retiro is a must-see that gives a rejuvenating respite from the bustle of the city.

Delving into Madrid's Rich History and Culture

Through its fusion of art, architecture, and customs that represent centuries of influence, Madrid's history and culture come to life. Every part of the city tells a story of Spain's creative accomplishments, regal past, and lively neighborhoods, making it seem like entering a living museum. Madrid is a place where the past and present coexist together, giving visitors a vibrant cultural experience that includes top-notch museums and ancient districts;

- **Casa de Campo**

Originally a royal hunting estate, Casa de Campo, Madrid's best green refuge from the hustle of the city, is a large park that stretches for kilometers of untouched nature with its rolling hills, streams, deep forests, and breathtaking vistas. There are many paths for running, cycling, and hiking, so this is a haven for those who like the outdoors and ensures visitors can engage in a variety of outdoor activities. The lovely lake in the park is perfect for a leisurely boat cruise; rentals are somewhat affordably priced. For those seeking leisure, shaded areas and lovely picnic grounds provide quiet times. Family holidays would be ideal in Casa de Campo because it has interesting attractions like an aquarium, zoo, and theme park. Accessible via the Lago metro station, Casa de Campo provides a mix of pristine environments and well-kept paths fit for all kinds of hikers.

Through the quiet rustle of dark fir trees as well as the dazzling glades bursting with lavender and wild chamomile, the natural beauty of the park is seductive. Visitors will find comfort in the water fountains and restaurants scattered along the paths within the park's expansive grounds.

- **Museo Nacional Centro de Arte Reina Sofía**

With pieces by notable painters like Picasso, Dalí, Miró, and Gris, the Museo Nacional Centro de Arte Reina Sofía is a true gold mine of Spanish art from the 20th century situated at *C. de Sta. Isabel, 52, Centro*. For art enthusiasts, it's an inexpensive cultural experience, with entrance costs from $11 and opening daily from 10 a.m. (except Tuesdays). Picasso's famed Guernica, a striking picture of the horrors of war, is displayed at the museum along with a substantial collection of surrealist and cubist paintings that track the history of modern art. In addition to paintings, the museum's exhibits contain sculpture, photography, graphic design, and even architectural displays, giving a thorough look at a variety of creative disciplines. Visitors should expect spending three hours or more examining its myriad treasures, which include political art and contemporary works dispersed across several levels of exhibitions.

It might be a bit difficult to traverse the museum's large layout, so it's advisable to purchase an audio guide or ask staff for help when you first arrive. Remember to buy tickets online to avoid possible long waits and enjoy a more smooth experience. In order to increase the visitor experience, the museum also includes clean amenities, lots of seating, and green places for relaxation.

- **Royal Site of San Lorenzo de El Escorial: Real Monasterio de San Lorenzo de El Escorial**

A monument to the beauty and cultural goals of Spain's Golden Age is the Royal Site of San Lorenzo de El Escorial, also called the Real Monasterio de San Lorenzo de El Escorial. This magnificent Renaissance structure at *Av Juan de Borbón y Battemberg, s/n, 28200 San Lorenzo de El Escorial*, was created between 1563 and 1584, and comprises a royal palace, church, library, monastery, pantheon, and school.

Each of these monuments is precisely created to reflect the creative and intellectual worldview of the period. Visitors are invited to examine its treasures that include a stunning domed library with over 40,000 ancient manuscripts and volumes, for entry ticket rates from $15 per person. The crypt is a melancholy burial site for Spain's kings and nobility, while the basilica, with its ornate embellishments, leaves visitors in awe. This UNESCO World Heritage Site is made even more enticing by the wide gardens that are perched on a slope with breathtaking perspectives. It is relatively close to Madrid, only a 40-minute train ride away, making it a wonderful day trip destination. With so many rooms and exhibitions, visitors should allow at least three hours to explore the complete site. Because of the intricate structure, remember to hire an audio guide or join a tour to make sure you don't miss any of the sights, such as the famed library or the royal apartments.

In some areas, like the Pantheon of Kings, photography is restricted, but the historical and artistic grandeur more than makes up for it. It is open every day from 10 a.m. (closed on Mondays), and in order to avoid enormous lineups, be sure to obtain tickets online. A journey to El Escorial gives the ability to observe the artistic and cultural triumphs of a particular period in addition to learning about Spanish history. After a day of touring, the nearby town is the perfect destination to unwind with its charming environment and regional delicacies.

- **Puerta de Alcalá**

Located at *Pl. de la Independencia, s/n, Retiro*, in the middle of Madrid's crowded Independence Square, stands the majestic neoclassical triumphal arch known as the Puerta de Alcalá. This magnificent monument was erected by Francesco Sabatini to replace a former 16th-century gate and was built between 1769 and 1778 during the reign of Charles III.

It today reflects the historical grandeur and architectural evolution of Madrid that was previously one of five gateways used by travelers from France, Aragon, and Catalonia to approach the walled city. The gate depicts Spain's path to modernity, and features five majestic gates adorned with gorgeous sculptures and precise stone carvings. The Puerta de Alcalá is located at a busy roundabout and is ringed by the active energy of the city, with small cafés, diners, and shopping nearby. Because of its location, it's an excellent spot to start your exploration of Madrid's historical and cultural monuments. Being open twenty-four hours a day, the Puerta de Alcalá is a stunning piece of art that invites people to take in its magnificence day or night. Its exquisite construction and powerful presence make it a must-see for everybody visiting Madrid. Its majesty has been restored by recent renovations, bringing out the great workmanship of its masonry once more. This monument is conveniently positioned in Retiro Park, is accessible from Retiro Metro Station and is great for a leisurely stroll or a photo op.

- **Royal Basilica of Saint Francis the Great: Real Basílica de San Francisco el Grande**

The Royal Basilica of Saint Francis the Great (Real Basílica de San Francisco el Grande) is a neoclassical gem and a treasure trove of Spanish art and history. Located at *C. de San Buenaventura, 1, Centro*, this enormous cathedral is home to one of the biggest domes in the world; the fourth highest in Europe, and stands as a tribute to architectural excellence. Originally erected on the site of a 13th-century Franciscan monastery, the basilica's huge dome and elaborate interiors attract visitors with their complex murals, including a masterpiece by the famed painter Francisco Goya. The inside displays a harmonic arrangement of sculptures of the twelve apostles ringing the nave, along with gorgeous shrines and altars that highlight remarkable workmanship. Visitors can marvel at the magnificent painted ceiling, an incredible show of workmanship that definitely demands to be experienced in person.

Access prices start at $5, and guided tours are offered for a deeper examination of its history and art collection, but certain mornings come with free access. The tranquil environment is typically heightened by quiet music, making the experience practically heavenly. Alongside its artistic riches, the basilica also holds a unique Christmas tableau in its foyer, giving a festive enchantment. The perfectly conserved murals, ornate shrines, and spectacular dome make this church a must-visit in

Madrid. Photography is allowed; but, flash is discouraged to maintain the integrity of the artwork.

- **National Archaeological Museum: Museo Arqueológico Nacional (MAN)**

With objects spanning from prehistoric to medieval times, the National Archaeological Museum, housed at *C. de Serrano, 13, Salamanca,* in a splendid neoclassical architecture, offers an enthralling historical tour. Cave art, Islamic pottery, Egyptian antiquities, Roman mosaics, and intricate Iberian sculptures are all part of the museum's extraordinary collection, which has garnered it a worldwide reputation.

Each part of the galleries gives an enthralling insight into the different civilizations that have affected Spain and the Mediterranean region, and visitors are escorted through them in an organized method. The spacious, light-filled halls create a tranquil setting that makes it simple to appreciate the richness and complexity of the museum's collections that vary from mundane things of ancient cultures to ceremonial treasures. The museum is open every day from 9:30 a.m. (closed on Mondays), and entrance is fairly priced, starting at $3 on certain days. Multimedia presentations and interactive displays augment the experience and give intriguing insights suited for all ages. The audio tour, which you can access on your phone, makes the visit more comfortable and thorough, and the treasure chamber, packed with beautiful gems and ceremonial objects, is a must-see highlight. Make time to visit this wonderful institution for at least three hours; it will give you a clearer appreciation of the inventiveness and resourcefulness of ancient cultures.

- **Museo del Romanticismo**

By means of its transportation of visitors to Madrid in the 19th century, the Museo del Romanticismo located at *C. de San Mateo, 13, Centro,* presents a glimpse into the charm, inventiveness, and daily life of the Romantic period. Housed in an 18th-century mansion, this modest and intriguing museum includes beautifully maintained rooms with rich furniture, artwork, and decorative objects evocative of a bygone age. Through the beautifully adorned ballroom with its gold-colored silk walls and shimmering chandeliers as well as the more utilitarian but gorgeous domestic quarters, every aspect of the museum transports visitors to a time when beauty and excess defined the European Romantic movement. Through its striking artwork, old toys, and personal items, the collection chronicles the nobles who once shaped Madrid's social and cultural landscape.

The museum's secret gem, the peaceful garden café, offers a quiet spot to relax after touring the house, but it could be closed for renovations sometimes. The Museo del Romanticismo, a moderately priced and educational attraction, offers free entrance on certain days and charges $3 per person. It is open every day except Monday and the perfect spot for a laid-back visit. It offers a close-up yet comprehensive perspective of this idealized historical age.

- **Teatro Real**

Captivating audiences since its opening in 1850, the Teatro Real, Spain's premier opera theater and pillar of the country's performing arts, this wonderful institution unites history, culture, and architectural splendor and is located at *Pl. de Isabel II, s/n, Centro,* adjacent to the Royal Palace in the middle of Madrid. With gilded balconies, a beautiful chandelier, and finely designed reception rooms, the theater's interior exhibits a regal grandeur, while its breathtaking façade overlooks attractive plazas and landscapes.

To get a closer look at the inventiveness and skill that define this monument, guests can take advantage of guided tours that allow access to its magnificent halls, rehearsal rooms, and the royal box. Note that it is essential to give preference to center seats for the greatest views of performances, the theater is also wheelchair accessible and features a speedy online ticketing system. With entry tickets starting from $8, this cultural jewel is astonishingly accessible. The Teatro

Real is a dynamic hub for art fans, with a wide roster of events that includes ballets, operas, and flamenco performances. The excellent acoustics and expertly picked actors make every play come to life, making witnessing a concert here an amazing experience. The shows that range from contemporary classics to timeless masterpieces like Madame Butterfly, are always of the greatest level.

An extra touch of elegance is provided to the evening during intermissions when guests can rest in nicely adorned rooms with royal pictures while enjoying pre-ordered snacks and drinks. The Salón de Baile regularly organizes innovative cultural events, like small-scale flamenco performances that showcase great local talent, for guests searching for a more immersive experience.

- **Real Jardín Botánico**

Situated at *Pl. Murillo, 2, Retiro*, the Real Jardín Botánico is a tranquil retreat complete with centuries of history and spectacular natural beauty. Founded in 1755 and transferred to its current position in 1781, this historic garden is recognized as a Spanish cultural property and is included in the

UNESCO-designated Landscape of Light. Across its broad grounds, the nation's greatest botanical garden displays a stunning blend of beautifully kept gardens, greenhouses, and walking routes. An affordable $4 entry ticket greets visitors and provides them access to a spectacular collection of plants presented on three finely tiered terraces. Carefully positioned sculptures and shaded walks add to the serene mood, and the garden's stunning display of flora includes both native Spanish species and exotic plants from all over the world.

A highlight is the modest bonsai terrace that shows neatly preserved little trees that demonstrate the skill of gardening. A visit to the Real Jardín Botánico is an experienced encounter in addition to being a visual feast. Constructed in 1856, this architecturally outstanding cast-iron greenhouse from the 19th century contains subtropical plants beneath its arching glass and iron roof. The greenhouse's temperature is now readily controlled, keeping its antique charm without losing comfort, owing to a clever manure-based heating system. In order to give guests a more cultural experience, the park also provides a selection of seasonal exhibitions, such as rotating showcases, photography shows, and works by area artists. It is the perfect destination for families and environment lovers alike due to the monthly activities and themed events that give extra possibilities for exploration and education. The Real Jardín Botánico offers a tranquil refuge in the center of the city, suitable for everyone desiring to come in touch with nature and history.

- **Parque Madrid Río**

Stretching along the banks of the Manzanares River, Parque Madrid Río situated at *P.º de la Ermita del Santo, 14, 16, Latina,* is a modern urban refuge with a huge and finely organized green space for visitors of all ages. The park is free to access, open 24 hours a day and has converted a bustling highway area into a tranquil refuge with lots of leisure activities. Walking, jogging, cycling, or relaxing on one of the countless seats strewn throughout are all made feasible by its linear shape. It is the perfect setting for families, athletes, and nature lovers, as it is flanked with well-kept gardens, sports fields, and playgrounds. In addition to historical gems like the Segovia Bridge and panoramic vistas of Madrid's cityscape, including the Royal Palace and Basilica, the park's beauty is complemented by splash pads and fountains, which give a refreshing touch during the warmer months. The Manzanares River's tranquil flow works as a unifying focal point and offers a pleasant backdrop for an outdoor day.

Adding to being a destination for pleasure, Parque Madrid Río is a focus for dynamic community life and cultural events. Enjoying a picnic by the river is made easier by the strategically situated cafés and neighboring grocers that give each visit a more comfortable air. The park's harmonic marriage of urban design and greenery reflects the city's devotion to sustainable regions while creating a quieter, cleaner ambiance away from the regular bustle of the metropolis. There are numerous sheltered locations for a break on a sunny day, and the sculptured pathways and bridges allow wandering at a leisurely pace.

Family-Friendly Activities

Madrid offers an array of family-friendly activities that blend culture, fun, and outdoor adventures, making it a fantastic destination for all ages. With fascinating museums, sprawling parks and unique experiences, there's something to keep everyone entertained;

- **Museo Nacional de Ciencias Naturales**

Visitors of all ages will enjoy an instructive experience at Madrid's Museo Nacional de Ciencias Naturales, a true gold mine of science, history, and biodiversity tucked at *C. de José Gutiérrez Abascal, 2, Chamartín*. The museum is one of the oldest scientific institutes in Europe and is situated in the former Palace of Arts and Industry, a 19th-century architectural masterpiece. King Carlos III created it in 1771, and it has since evolved into a cutting-edge center for natural scientific study. Fossils, taxidermy, dinosaur reconstructions, and a magnificent mineral display are all part of its extensive collection. The bones of Megatherium americanum, which are historically notable for being the first to be discovered in a fixed anatomical position, are among its highlights. While the space-themed exhibits and geological displays give a broader understanding of our planet and beyond, the giant whale skeleton and the famed dioramas representing Earth's biodiversity capture the imagination. This museum is engaging and enlightening, particularly for families and youngsters, owing to its interactive displays and well-organized exhibits.

With the assistance of immersive videos and models that bring the science to life, guests can explore halls that cover themes such as Charles Darwin's pioneering work, extinction events, and human evolution. The usage of 3D-printed models that ensure accessibility for persons with limited vision, is a remarkable feature. A unique view of Earth's history can also be acquired via the museum's outdoor geology gardens and minor meteorite collection. It is a cost-effective and satisfying visit, as tickets are from 7 euros per person, with student discounts available.

- **Parque de Atracciones de Madrid**

Madrid's premier urban theme park, Parque de Atracciones, provides a choice of adrenaline adventures, fun for the entire family, and fantastic live entertainment. All ages will enjoy the park's more than 30 attractions, scattered across numerous themed zones. Rides like Tarántula, a spinning coaster that delivers intense adrenaline, and Abismo, a twisting roller coaster with huge drops, are excellent for thrill-seekers. The Walking Dead Experience is a riveting and disturbing trip for lovers of horror.

Gentle rides, vivid carousels, and amusing water features are suitable for families with tiny children and are a terrific way to cool off during the summer. The park's wonderful design, with trees giving shade and well-kept trails, makes it easy to roam around and soak in the vivid atmosphere. With moderately budget friendly entrance costs starting at $24 per person, Parque de Atracciones is an excellent alternative for a day trip and is only available on weekends. Transportation is hassle-free owing to its excellent location in Casa de Campo and simple access via Madrid's Metro and bus services. Park refreshments might be pricey, so guests should take their own snacks and water bottles. There are plenty of family amenities and separate prayer places for persons with special needs. Wait times for attractions are fewer during slower seasons, such as the winter, so visitors can take advantage of everything the park has to offer.

- **Naval Museum: Museo Naval**

From Isabella and Ferdinand's dominion to modern maritime activities, the history of the Spanish navy is fascinatingly recounted at the Museo Naval de Madrid, or Naval Museum. Housed at *P.º del Prado, 3, Retiro,* in a wonderfully restored historic edifice, this museum is a genuine treasure mine of shipbuilding, naval science, and international adventure. Open Tuesday through Sunday from 10:00 a.m. to 7:00 p.m. (and until 3:00 p.m. in August), it gives a fascinating view of how Spain came to dominance in the nautical world. Visitors get to explore an outstanding collection of antiques, exquisite ship models, nautical artwork, and ancient weaponry for an optional donation of €3. The exhibitions are structured chronologically, taking visitors from the 15th-century wooden sailing ships to modern naval ships. All can observe each exhibit as it comes with explanations in both Spanish and English. The museum's remarkable collection of ship models, which are exquisitely detailed and depict the progress of maritime engineering over the years, is its principal attraction.

Admire the beautifully restored captain's quarters, vintage navigational aids, and spectacular artwork that represents major naval discoveries and wars. The museum is entertaining and instructional for families, especially older youngsters interested in history and technology, even if there are no interactive exhibits. It is an excellent replacement for Madrid's big museums because of its tranquil setting and lots of things to explore at a leisurely pace.

- **Matadero Madrid**

Matadero Madrid is a spectacular cultural institution built in a charmingly refurbished former slaughterhouse at *Pl. de Legazpi, 8, Arganzuela,* that serves as a hub for contemporary art, innovation, and community participation. This vast industrial structure, located alongside Madrid Río Park, has been turned into a dynamic center that offers workshops, art exhibitions, theatrical plays, movie screenings, and more.

The avant-garde and experimental displays dispersed across various locations are inspired by the building's unusual red-brick architecture. The bulk of the exhibits allow free entrance, although others are still very moderately priced, making it a cultural destination that is readily accessible. Along with open public spaces where visitors can rest, observe exhibitions, or join in seasonal events, the complex also features the Cineteca, a unique cinema specialized in independent and experimental films. In addition to being a refuge for art enthusiasts, Matadero also welcomes families, artists, and curious travelers. Children can run around freely in its spacious grounds, and bikes may be rented to explore the area. Visitors get to also enjoy a food or a drink at the terrace bar after taking in one of the various exhibits, featuring immersive installations and current visual arts. The area also includes comfy nooks and WiFi. Matadero is a brilliant example of urban redevelopment, masterfully integrating its industrial past with a modern, inclusive vision of creation.

- **Greenhouse Crystal Palace of Arganzuela: Invernadero del Palacio de Cristal de Arganzuela**

A beautiful glass and metal edifice erected in 1887, the Invernadero del Palacio de Cristal de Arganzuela is a horticultural jewel nestled away in the Madrid Río area. With its four unique environments; subtropical, two tropical, and a dry region with cactus and succulents, this gorgeous greenhouse is an amazing destination to learn about the diversity of plant life from throughout the world. Everyone, including those in wheelchairs and strollers, can visit owing to the well-thought-out ramps, and entrance is free. With complicated orchids as well as odd tree trunks with otherworldly shapes, each location features flora that have been deliberately kept to suit their unique climates. Some of the unusual and remarkable species are on show. There are no digital guides or QR codes, but educational placards that offer information on the featured flora are put near the exhibitions. The location is tranquil and uncrowded, making it perfect for a pleasant vacation in nature, particularly in the morning.

Beyond its botanical wonders, the greenhouse is a piece of beauty in terms of design, with big glass panels that allow in an abundance of natural light. It's a great area to wander, rest on a seat, and appreciate the surrounding lush environment due to the tranquil mood. While the tropical zones are overflowing with beautiful flora that transport you to other locations, the desert area is known for its incredible array of cacti and succulents. This greenhouse offers a fascinating mix of nature and history, making it a fantastic option for educational expeditions, tranquil leisure spaces, or revitalizing activities for both kids and adults. It's a nice location to stop if you're seeing Madrid Río or need a break from the hustle of the city and it is open every day except Mondays from 10 AM to 2 PM.

CULINARY EXPERIENCES, NIGHTLIFE AND ENTERTAINMENT

Traditional Tapas Tour

A lovely way to experience the local food and culture is to go on a traditional tapas tour in Madrid. These experiences take you around the city's lively districts and give you the opportunity to sample a range of real Spanish tapas, like patatas bravas, jamón ibérico, fresh seafood, and regional cheeses. You will experience the history and importance of these meals as well as the vibrant ambiance of Madrid's culinary scene as you visit several historic taverns. A tapas tour is ideal for foodies since it blends delicious dishes with regional tales while taking in Madrid's vibrant atmosphere:

- **Bodega de la Ardosa**

Famous for its intimate setting, timeless charm, and food full of true Spanish flavors, Bodega de la Ardosa is a well-liked tapas tavern located at *C. de Colón, 13, Centro*. This laid-back setting in the midst of the city is excellent for a night of scrumptious appetizers and cold drinks. It's easy to enjoy a range of typical Spanish tapas, with portions costing between 10 and 20 euros. Highlights include the legendary tortilla, widely recognized as one of the greatest in the city, and the thick and savory jamón. A must-try is the croquette, particularly the house-made carabiniere variety known for its taste and delicate texture. The bar at Bodega de la Ardosa is regularly full, creating a bustling environment. The service is nevertheless polite and efficient in spite of its popularity, ensuring that guests enjoy a spotless stay.

The bar's ability in traditional Spanish food is further displayed by the delectable Carrillera de Buey Estofada, a beef stew. The cheesecake is a fantastic way to end off a supper because it finds the appropriate mix between sweetness and richness. Also not to be missed is the vermouth that is available on tap, that gives your experience an added touch of regional character.

- **El Sur de Moratín**

Tucked at *C. de Moratín, 19, Centro*, El Sur de Moratín is a charming, traditional Spanish tavern (taberna tradicional española) that provides a large range of authentic cuisine at prices between 10 and 20 euros each. The restaurant is well-known for its pleasant environment and scrumptious, freshly cooked dishes that emphasize the greatest Spanish cuisine. Highlights include the excellent garlic shrimp and the amply portioned, moist, and flavorful paella.

Another favorite is the grilled octopus, recognized for being tender and expertly cooked, and the shrimp risotto that delivers an unsurpassed creamy, pleasing flavor. This warm, energetic restaurant is open every day and is a terrific alternative for those looking to dine in a laid-back atmosphere. The space can get a bit crowded, but the plush seating contributes to the room's intimate charm. Visitors will enjoy a smooth experience thanks to the staff's swift and polite service and fluency in English.

- **La Vaca y La Huerta**

La Vaca y La Huerta is a hidden gem set at *C. de Recoletos, 7, Salamanca,* combining modern design with rustic appeal. Covered with exposed brickwork and industrial elements, this chic restaurant specializes in excellent meats and seasonal vegetarian cuisine. With prices between thirty and fifty euros for each dish, it offers a gourmet experience combining the finest cuts of beef with fresh produce directly from their garden. Here, the focus is on employing meticulous preparation to make powerful, real flavors.

Signature dishes include the fresh escalope oozing with blue cheese from northern Spain and the masterfully cooked entrecôte, known for its sumptuous, fatty richness. Though the Wagyu beef and beef tartare are soft, tasty nibbles, the "ugly" tomato salad, dressed with olive oil and black salt, is an interesting appetizer. Because of its vegetarian options; artichokes and leeks, which emphasize its dedication to utilizing seasonal, fresh foods, the restaurant is a must-visit for both meat eaters and vegetarians. Given its friendly atmosphere and first-rate service, La Vaca y La Huerta, open Wednesday through Saturday, is ideal for small dinner groups or get-togethers. There are generous servings and thoughtful touches, like complimentary soup and certain dishes made right at the table, that improve the dining experience. Pair your dinner with a glass of Rioja or another carefully selected wine to perfectly balance the flavors. The luscious cheesecake is a rich and satisfying way to cap a supper, and dessert enthusiasts won't want to miss it. Be sure to reserve tickets in advance as it always fills up.

- **Casa Revuelta**

Located at *C. de Latoneros, 3, Centro*, Casa Revuelta is a classic Spanish tavern that is well-known for its traditional and true Spanish food. Founded by Santiago Revuelta in 1966, this popular restaurant is well-known for its fried fish, or "tajada de bacalao," as it is called locally. The cod is regarded to be the finest supper in Madrid because it is juicy, suitably seasoned, and wrapped in a golden, crispy batter. In addition to its well-known cod, Casa Revuelta provides a range of tapas that are created fresh to order using quality ingredients, like substantial Madrid-style tripe stew, creamy croquettes, and crisp pig cracklings. This eatery delivers wonderful flavors at moderate prices, with meals running between €10 and €20. For the ideal tapas experience, accompany them with a glass of vermouth or a cool beer.

Casa Revuelta offers a dynamic, crowded air, and customers typically dine while standing at the counter or squeezed into odd corners. Even during busy periods, guests are assured a flawless eating experience thanks to the efficient and friendly service. The flavors that await make the wait worthwhile, even if there isn't much seating. The menu's focus is the salted fish, but scrumptious accompaniments include artichokes, their cheesecake dessert, and broken eggs with ham and Padron peppers. Open every day except Tuesdays, this historic gem of Madrid's culinary scene is a must-see for everyone searching for an authentic Spanish taste in a relaxed, welcoming setting.

- **Malaspina: Taberna Malaspina**

A classic tapas bar with a touch of Spanish charm, Taberna Malaspina is nestled at *C. de Cádiz, 9, Centro,* and is a friendly taverna well-known for its pleasant environment that delivers the ultimate Madrid dining experience with its rustic décor, welcoming service, and scrumptious cuisine. The menu comprises a range of heavy shared platters and traditional tapas, with pricing generally between €10 and €20 per dish.

Popular alternatives created with fresh, quality ingredients include baby squid, tortilla tapas, fried peppers, and jamón. The drinks menu, which includes house-made sangria, cold mojitos, and a moderately priced but tasty choice of wines, is also exceptional. Free tapas are served with every drink, adding to its charm and giving guests another taste of true Spanish food. A nice experience is ensured even during busy hours thanks to the attentive service and inviting, energetic environment. The taverna attracts both locals and visitors due to its rustic and humble feel despite its prominent location. Guests are made to feel entirely at home by the cheerful and helpful bar staff.

Must-Visit Restaurants and Must-Eats

Madrid would be a bright, flavorful feast with a wealth of charm if it were a dish. The city's culinary culture is as robust, diversified, and unapologetically great as its spirit. There is a dish and a narrative at every turn, with hidden gems where abuelas continue to stir the pot as well as modern eateries redefining Spanish cuisine. Here's your foodie must visit list, no repeats, no regrets:

- **Angelita Madrid**

A culinary jewel that reinvents current Spanish cuisine, Angelita Madrid is nestled away at *C. de la Reina, 4*. Every facet of this delightful, modest treasure; the broad wine selection and the locally made food, has been meticulously picked. Food and wine enthusiasts should make time to visit Angelita, which is only open Monday through Friday beginning at 5:00 PM. With a cuisine full of vibrant flavors and seasonal creations, the crew, who are recognized for their immaculate service, makes sure every guest feels like a treasured friend. Dishes like the delicate pulpo (octopus), beautifully seasoned pork and inventive cannelloni, exhibits the expertise and attention to detail that distinguish this restaurant. However, the food is only one component of the enchantment. Angelita features a cocktail bar underneath that is an experience in and of itself, as well as an outstanding wine selection that originates from their family's farm near Zamora.

Forget about the standard ice cubes and wasted pours; this bar employs innovation and precision to increase mixology, making each sip an experience. You can imagine it's just another establishment due to the inconspicuous design, but the mood and tastes quickly make you realise that's not the case. Pro tip: *You'll want to indulge in numerous foods or beverages, so reserve room for a second round.*

- **Casa Dani**

A Madrid culinary classic recognized for its colorful flavors and real Mediterranean charm, Casa Dani is situated at *Cl. de Ayala,* in the crowded Mercado de la Paz. This is a go-to location for hearty Spanish classics served with excellent ingredients and a handmade touch, a long-running counter that is open Monday through Saturday from 8 AM. Their light, fluffy tortilla de patatas, which are filled with the sweet, caramelized flavor of onions, are clearly the showstopper. It should come as no surprise that Casa Dani offers "The Best Tortilla in Spain." You can enjoy a fantastic range of traditional tapas like croquettes, garlic prawns, and beautiful lamb chops, as well as exotic meals like grilled pig ear and soft oxtail, with menu prices running from €10 to €20 per item.

Casa Dani's versatility; you can order from the comfort of your home via Uber Eats, grab a meal for takeaway, or enjoy a casual dine-in experience so that it is even more exceptional. **Fun fact:** Casa Dani's family farm produces a majority of the ingredients, assuring each dish's unsurpassed freshness. The inviting atmosphere is maintained by the cheerful crew, and it is well liked by both residents and tourists. A professional tip? While it's common and entertaining to wait at one of the outdoor kiosks for a quick lunch, avoid peak hours (1-2 PM) to avoid the massive queues. Don't forget to complete your meal with a slice of their creamy cheesecake or complement the tortilla with their famed bread.

- **Rosi La Loca**

Enter Rosi La Loca, a maximalist, colorful utopia at *C. de Cádiz,* where traditional Spanish food and innovative tapas merge with an imaginative, Alice-in-paradise ambiance. This vibrant restaurant opens every day from 12:30 PM, focusing as much on the experience as the food. The menu offers a feast of flavors and ingenuity, with meals costing between €20 and €40. Every meal, including their tacos, bao buns, and the renowned squid paella, is delivered on beautifully creative crockery that makes every bite a picture-perfect moment. Don't miss their innovative drinks or homemade sangria, which are both nicely crafted to match with the various food. When a meal of udon noodles or a tiramisu is given to you in a small cafetera, it's hard not to smile. You feel as if you've slipped down a rabbit hole into a gastronomic wonderland owing to the decor's brilliant colors, floral embellishments, and strange touches. The magic is increased by the courteous, welcoming people, who make sure every visit is nothing short of fantastic. **Pro tip:** As this treasure fills up swiftly, reservations should be made to avoid disappointment. The menu's selected selections make sure every meal is worthwhile even if you're pushed for time.

Fun fact: Rosi La Loca takes joy in mixing the traditional with the contemporary, putting a unique touch on classic Spanish foods like patatas bravas and tortillas. You will remember it long after you have left Madrid because it is a celebration of flavor and ingenuity. Let the rainbow of tastes and sights do the talking instead of you taking our word for it.

- **Sacha Restaurant: Restaurante Sacha**

Since 1972, visitors have been thrilled by Restaurante Sacha, a gourmet gem concealed behind a simple blue door at *Zona ajardinada, C. de*

Juan Hurtado de Mendoza. With a setting that takes you back in time, this modest café effectively mixes the flavors of Galician and Basque cuisine. Particularly in the summer, its snug dining space and small courtyard patio are excellent for savoring a leisurely meal. The menu is only accessible in Spanish, revealing a focus on utilizing only the finest ingredients and excellent preparation. Lamb chops, stingray in black butter, and the Falsa Lasagna de Txangurro; a crab-based "false lasagna" are some of the features that make the dinner very outstanding. The bone marrow and sweetbreads are must-tries for everyone who appreciates robust flavors.

The delicate skate melts in your mouth as well as the soft omelet with blood sausage and crisp potatoes, each presented with perfection. Dining at Sacha is a holistic experience packed with artistry and history, and it's not just about the meal. With its ancient furniture and walls that vibrate with decades' worth of stories, the ambiance is quietly wonderful. Even when the service could be a touch sluggish at times, it merely heightens the experience's unrushed enchantment. Be sure to make your reservation well in advance, as this tiny space fills up rapidly, a few lucky customers might be able to take advantage of same-day cancellations. **Fun fact:** Sacha is famous for greeting tourists with kindness, which contributes to the personal environment of the restaurant, which was named after the parents' only son.

- **Riveira do Miño**

Tucked at *Calle de Sta. Brígida,,* Riveira do Miño is a seafood lovers delight that conveys Galicia to the capital. This friendly cafe brings you to a world where fresh seafood is king, replete with nautical décor and pictures. The meals on the menu are a celebration of crustáceos (crustaceans) and mariscos (shellfish) that go well with crisp Galician wines like Albariño or Ribeiro. A flavor of traditional Galician comfort food can be found in substantial dishes like lacón con grelos and freshly baked empanadas, while the famed pulpo a la gallega (Galician-style octopus) is a must-try, as it is soft and beautifully seasoned. Every meal is proof of their devotion to authenticity and quality. Bring your hunger (and maybe a few companions to share the wealth) as the servings are generous, seriously; the seafood dish for two may easily fill three or four ravenous diners. With items priced between €30 and €40, the prices are modest and give exceptional value for such high-quality seafood.

It is the perfect venue for get-togethers with friends due to its colorful mood, filled with laughter and the sound of shells clinking. Since this eatery fills up rapidly, book a reservation in advance, especially if you're coming during popular meal hours. Also, be ready to get your hands dirty; a lot of de-shelling is necessary, but that's all part of the fun. **Here's a "fun" fact**: the seafood at the restaurant is so fresh that it feels like it just jumped onto your platter from the ocean.

- **El Club Allard | Restaurante Estrella Michelin**

Enter the world of El Club Allard, where each dish appears like an invitation to an incredible trip and where cooking becomes art. This Michelin-starred restaurant situated at *C. de Ferraz, 2, Moncloa - Aravaca,* is a visual and gastronomic feast, located in an artistically constructed structure. Overhead, chandeliers shimmer as the magnificent ambiance envelops you, preparing you for a gourmet adventure that is as imaginative as it is indulgent. Spanish gastronomy with worldwide influences is highlighted in the tasting menus varying from 10 to 12 courses. Imagine nori with lobster that tastes like a kiss from the sea, or Iberian pork shoulder served with mustard ice cream; each dish is as lovely to look at as it is to eat. The experience is further enhanced by carefully chosen wines that bring out the particular features of each dish.

Be prepared to spend at least €100, but the superb quality and attention to detail make every cent justified. The cuisine is innovative and engaging, and surprises like edible cards and liquid nitrogen-made desserts give the supper a theatrical aspect. Leave aside at least three hours to properly appreciate this experience; it's a gourmet symphony, so be sure to take your time. A group of attentive staff members is ready to explain to you the menu in either Spanish or English, and the service is equally as sophisticated as the food. **Fun fact:** the chef frequently recounts the background of the meals, and that increases the immersive experience. The restaurant's philosophy is to merge the originality of its cuisine with the bounty of nature.

- **El Paraguas**

Tucked at *C. de Jorge Juan,* in one of Madrid's most wealthy areas, El Paraguas presents a fantastic Asturian gastronomic experience that marries elegance and tradition. This exquisite café is well-known for its traditional foods, such as solomillo de ternera (fried veal with ham and cheese) and fabada asturiana (bean stew), which are served in a setting as beautiful as the food. Imagine dining in a pleasant atmosphere with great décor and the ability to sit on a gorgeous patio that is covered by glass. Every part of your visit is methodically organized; starting with the expertly picked wine selection down to the artistically placed foods that nearly beg for consumption. Each meal combines powerful flavors with a contemporary twist, paying attention to quality and tradition. Sample the lobster rice or verdinas con perdiz (tiny green beans with partridge), they have become popular meals.

This place is perfect for gatherings or small lunches because of the environment that fosters extended, leisurely discussions. The service is discrete and personable, complementing the beautiful experience. **Fun fact:** Even seasoned diners are astonished by the cheesy twist of the butter served with bread. Take advantage of the daily offers if they are given. Simple but brimming with flavor, the off-menu lenguado (sole fish) is a hidden gem. Although El Paraguas is undoubtedly more costly, the excellent execution, atmosphere, and sincerity make the price justified. If the weather permits, pick outdoor eating to soak in the bustling neighborhood scene and visit early to explore the gorgeous street outside.

Madrid's culinary soul is a mix of tradition and experimentation. Whatever you do, leave room for churros, take your time with tapas, and never underestimate the power of a well-poured vermouth to make every bite taste just a little better.

Flamenco Shows

Madrid is a hub of flamenco amid a flurry of stomping feet, clapping hands, and soul-stirring songs where passion, rhythm, and unadulterated emotion meet. Witnessing a flamenco concert here is nothing short of seeing a sort of art so strong that it looks like it would burn the room down. Through the intimate environment of a tablao and bigger venues, Flamenco in Madrid is a visceral experience that will inspire you to yell "¡Olé!" (trust me, it's encouraged).

A tip: Sit close to the stage to feel every heel hit and watch the dancer's eyes glitter. Get some appetizers and a glass of Spanish wine to really savor the event. Flamenco is more than just dance; did you realize that? Originating in Andalusian, Gypsy, and Moorish traditions, it is a blending of intricate rhythms, guitar playing, and vocals. And whatever your expertise level might be, a night at a flamenco performance will leave you in awe, and you could even find yourself marching back to the venue (it's harder than it sounds);

- **Cardamomo Tablao Flamenco**

Through the exhilarating art of flamenco, Madrid's vivid spirit comes to life at Cardamomo Tablao Flamenco located at *Calle de Echegaray*. Considered one of the best flamenco experiences available worldwide, this modest theater hidden in the middle of the city has captivated spectators since 1994. It is a stage with dancers, singers, and musicians performing with undiluted passion and exhilarating intensity, surrounded by comfy chairs and soothing lighting.

Every pluck, stomp, and emotional sound made captivates you totally. The show is a passionate homage to Spanish culture, replete with poignant melodies and powerful dancing. With daily performances and entry ticket rates starting at roughly $41 or €39, it's a worthy treat for everyone wishing to experience the genuine essence of Spain. A delightful part of the experience is the provision of a welcome drink, which can be wine, sangria, or any other form of refreshment. Cardamomo pulls you to the vivid core of flamenco, you will be awed by the flowing dresses and beating your feet to the rhythmic claps. Every seat feels close to the action because of the venue's tiny and efficient design. You can choose to enjoy a formal meal in advance to get the most out of your evening, so you may enjoy the show with Spanish tapas. For a post-dinner experience that enables you to absorb the magic without rushing, opt for the 9:00 PM or 10:30 PM show. **Fun fact:** The New York Times promotes Cardamomo as the lone flamenco venue in Madrid, and for good reason. This business is as authentic as it gets, having been established for almost 30 years, and is a must-visit for both new and veteran flamenco fans.

- **FLAMENCO Las Tablas: Tablao Flamenco Las Tablas**

Flamenco Tablao situated at *Pl. de España, 9, Moncloa,* is a place where innovation and history collide. Established more than two decades ago by two forward-thinking dancers, Antonia Moya and Marisol Navarro, this venue elevates flamenco to a new level with its contemporary architecture and unparalleled stage; the biggest for flamenco performances in Madrid. Every stomp, pluck, and passionate note in this performance is infused with love, creating an enthralling spectacle that is both intimate and majestic. Every day at 7:00 PM and 9:30 PM, performances highlight the unadulterated talent of musicians, dancers, and singers who give their all to every moment. Las Tablas is the ideal place for a fully immersed cultural experience since it serves excellent traditional Spanish food and an amazing wine selection if you're in the mood for a bit of extra decadence. While the $47 (€45) entry tickets can seem like a lot of money, be assured that the memories you'll make there are invaluable.

Las Tablas's charm is found in both its small venue and its top-notch performances. The actors almost seem to be inviting you into their tale because of how close they are to the stage, making every hand gesture, foot swivel, and emotional note seem intimate. No two performances are ever the same, so expect a concert full of improvisation, emotion, and skill. Be sure to get a sangria before the concert if you're going on a hot summer day. It's refreshing and gives your evening a little Spanish flavor. **Fun fact:** Flamenco is a live art form with strong roots in Spanish history that is recognized by UNESCO as a cultural heritage. So attending a performance at Las Tablas is a spiritual experience that will leave you feeling touched, inspired, and completely enthralled.

- **Café Ziryab: Tablao Flamenco Café Ziryab**

Enter the mesmerizing world of flamenco at Café Ziryab, a hidden treasure located at *P.º de la Esperanza, 17, Arganzuela*, where intimacy, passion, and tradition are prized strongly. Close to the stage, this pleasant tablao is a favorite place for flamenco fans, enabling you to completely immerse yourself in the lyrical art form. At $35 (€33) for entry tickets, the experience enjoyed here is a wonderful price. With their captivating guitar strum, their moving voice and their rhythmic tapping of the dancers' heels, every performance is an engrossing demonstration

84

of undiluted skill. Designed to make you feel like a welcome guest at a flamenco family gathering, the location itself is a wonderful retreat from the hectic city. The sangria, too? Perfect for establishing the atmosphere and refreshingly on target. Here every seat appears like the nicest in the house thanks to the cosy positioning that ensures a close-up view of the performers' enthusiasm and intensity. An extra element of pleasure is supplied by the staff's friendly greeting, and that makes it evident that they love sharing this colorful habit. Get there a little early to secure the best seat, have a drink, and soak in the scene.

Fun fact: Although flamenco started in Andalusia, it has made Madrid its second home, with both classic and avant-garde performances at locations like Café Ziryab. This tablao offers a memorable evening. It's equal parts moving and thrilling, with a tinge of drama. After all, without a little fire, flamenco wouldn't be flamenco.

- **Tablao Villa - Rosa**

One of the world's oldest and most recognized flamenco theaters, Tablao Villa-Rosa at *C. de Núñez de Arce*, welcomes you to join a world of passion and history. A spectacular evening of music, dancing, and Spanish culture is given by this tablao located in a historic structure with stunning architecture inspired by Andalusia. You will enter the heart of flamenco, an art form that elicits raw emotion unlike any other, as the lights go down and the rhythmic tapping of heels fills the air. Dancers, singers, and musicians give their all to each move, note, and strum in these performances, and they are nothing short of fascinating. What's the best part? No matter where you sit, you will surely be a part of the magic, as every seat in the house offers a spectacular view.

The performances at Tablao Villa-Rosa are remarkable as is the service. From booking your reservation until you take your last cup of sangria, the staff is friendly and makes sure your evening goes well. Be sure to verify your reservation one more time to avoid any mix ups, and attempt to register far in advance to assure the nicest seats because front-row tickets are absolutely worth the money. **Fun fact:** This site is considered the world's oldest flamenco tablao, which gives your experience an added degree of authenticity. Villa-Rosa is a cultural gem that creates an effect by giving you the option of enjoying some tapas, a complimentary drink and at the same time, soaking in the exhilarating environment. Before the final curtain call, you might find yourself making arrangements for your next visit. This style of flamenco has the capacity to captivate your heart.

- **Teatro Flamenco Madrid**

Teatro Flamenco Madrid nestled at *C. del Pez,* is the place to go for a wonderful experience of Spain's cultural hub. This prime flamenco experience that takes place in a tiny, charming theater, brings the beauty of dance, song, and the iconic Spanish guitar to life in front of you. Some of the most skilled flamenco artists in the country give performances that blend scorching passion and profound musicianship. The soul-stirring world of flamenco is widely accessible, with tickets starting at $30 or €29. No matter where you sit, you can immerse yourself in the engaging footwork, enchanting songs, and compelling narrative because every seat in the house offers a wonderful view. And the vigor, too? Simply amazing; you will find yourself cheering without even realizing it. The potential of Teatro Flamenco Madrid to immerse you in the essence of this ancient art form is among its outstanding attributes. With solos, duets, and group performances that showcase the dancers' precision and the musicians' ingenuity, the one-hour program strikes the appropriate balance.

Fun fact: This is one of Madrid's most renowned flamenco venues, and it blends traditional performances with a splash of current flavor. To secure the nicest general seats and a complimentary drink with your ticket, be sure to arrive 20 minutes early. It's all part of the experience, so for an additional treat, relax at a table and enjoy the scene while sipping sangria.

- **Flamenco Essential Flamenco Show: Teatro Tablao Flamenco TORERO · Essential Flamenco**

This Flamenco Show theatre exudes a vibe of entering an ancient brick basement where each pluck, clap, and stomp carries a sense of heritage and passion. Without microphones or other distractions, this is flamenco at its most basic; pure creativity delivered within arm's length. The location itself is enchanted; located at *C. de la Cruz,* it's a warm subterranean area that transports you back to the beginnings of this well-known Spanish art form. The hour-long performance, which starts at $40(€39), takes viewers on a trip through the strong emotions of flamenco, including love, joy, grief, and passion, all of which are interwoven in a captivating performance.

El Mistela's creative supervision of the program guarantees that each moment is infused with genuineness. The performers, who include singers, guitarists, dancers, and even a cajón player, put on a powerful and very intimate show. The experience is enhanced by the small setting of the venue; every beat of the dancers' deft footwork will make the floor vibrate under your feet. **Fun fact:** this brick basement is a contemporary homage to the caverns where flamenco concerts such as this one were formerly staged. Get there early for a free drink, like a cool sangria that goes well with the flaming act.

Trendy Rooftop Bars with Stunning Views

Unquestionably, there's a certain allure to enjoying a martini while the metropolitan skyline unfolds in front of you. Trendy rooftop bars make for the ideal combination of stunning views, delectable beverages, and an atmosphere that transports you to a movie set. They are the meeting point of elegance and sunsets. Madrid is no exception; you can hang out with friends or sneak in a romantic date, either way the city's rooftop culture is teeming with places that allow you to experience its appeal from above.

Plan your visit around golden hour, when the light is stunning for Instagram and the ambiance is as golden as your beverage. Look out for those little additions that turn an already fantastic event into something really memorable, such as rooftop pools or live music performances. You may enjoy a little of history while sipping your mojito on the roofs of several of Madrid's ancient buildings. So where should you go next to see those breathtaking views?

- **Ginkgo Restaurante & Sky Bar**

Ginkgo Restaurante & Sky Bar is a hidden gem tucked high above the well-known Plaza de España in Madrid's heart. Along with amazing views, this stylish rooftop spot has a vibrant gastronomic scene. The menu offers a broad selection of alternatives like classic Spanish cooking, inventive international dishes and Asian-inspired specialties. Imagine strong sushi rolls, Mediterranean classics with a contemporary twist, and even crowd-pleasing meals like gourmet burgers.

The terrace's elegant but pleasant setting is great for soaking in the 270-degree views while sipping beautifully crafted drinks. You're in for a treat whether you're planning a romantic supper outdoors or a sunny lunch, as it opens at 1 PM every day. With club nights and live performances every Saturday from 10 PM to 2 AM, Ginkgo takes things to the next level when the weekend comes, giving your evening a glossy touch. The huge outdoor patio is the best setting for daytime or evening cityscape photography as it features comfy seating and panoramic glass walls. A DJ keeps the vibe lively inside, and the contemporary décor offers a sophisticated environment for your gastronomic adventure. To assure your space, particularly during busy seasons, make a reservation. The elevator ride up costs €4 per person, which is a reasonable fee to pay for such a spectacular view and fantastic experience. Here's some fascinating information to impress your fellow diners. The tenderloin steak and spicy salmon rolls are two menu highlights that blend well with the setting of this must-see rooftop sanctuary.

- **Nice To Meet You Restaurant & Lounge**

The 14th floor of the contemporary Dear Hotel is home to the cosmopolitan gem Nice To Meet You Restaurant & Lounge, which provides spectacular 360° panoramic views of Madrid. The city extends out in front of you from its modern terrace, offering the perfect setting for a wonderful supper. This sophisticated restaurant at *Gran Vía,* offers contemporary cuisine that cleverly mixes powerful flavors and fresh ingredients, and is open every day beginning at 12 PM. With delights like savory oxtail lasagna, exquisite grilled octopus, and artichoke dishes that steal the stage, the menu provides a remarkable combination of Mediterranean and Spanish-inspired food. Plus, the desserts are superb, notably their variation of tiramisu. Enjoy a glass of wine or one of their delicious cocktails with your dinner while watching the city lights or sunset. Not only is the food what makes Nice To Meet You distinctive, but the overall experience is complemented by the wonderful environment and impeccable service.

The location offers a stylish and laid-back air, both inside or on the terrace in the breeze. For a special occasion, a romantic meal, or maybe a tranquil evening of indulgence, the outdoor seating is excellent. A professional piece of advice? It's the romance of the golden hour paired with exquisite food that makes this place a must-visit, so secure your table in advance, especially for sunset dining. **Fun fact:** The terrace bar is a popular spot for unique, funky music that enriches the experience, so it's not just about the views.

- **La Terraza de Óscar**

    Perched above the Room Mate Óscar Hotel in the bustling Chueca district, La Terraza de Óscar is a place where city flair meets rooftop dreams. This contemporary cocktail bar is open all year round and boasts panoramic views of the Madrid skyline, making it the ideal spot to grab a drink and soak in the excitement of the city. This bar offers evening cocktails as well as a Saturday brunch (which is served from 12:30 to 3:00 PM), and you'll be greeted by a sophisticated yet pleasant environment that comprises a heated indoor room and an outside patio.

Its menu, which includes delightful cocktails, a beautifully picked array of small appetizers, and meals that vary in price from €10 to €20, hits the optimum blend of elegance and affordability. As Madrid transitions from day to night, it's like witnessing the city create its own masterpiece as you watch the sunset from this rooftop. The views aren't the only thing that stand out. These beverages are creative masterpieces, prepared with flair and a little bit of ingenuity. You can make the perfect evening by providing your drink with some tiny appetizers. This rooftop beauty tends to fill up quickly, so get there early to snag the nicest table for sunset. To reserve your position for a leisurely start to your weekend, make a reservation if you wish to attend brunch.

Fun fact: The terrace is a good place to people-watch from above because it overlooks Plaza de Pedro Zerolo, one of Chueca's liveliest squares.

- **Doña Luz Restaurante: Doñaluz The Madrid Rooftop**

Perched elegantly at *C. de la Montera,* on a rooftop near Madrid's iconic Puerta del Sol, Doña Luz Restaurante is a culinary treasure that serves food that is as excellent and cosmopolitan as its breathtaking views. With its beautiful décor with South American elements and its huge terrace where diners can enjoy vast city views, the restaurant's setting is a vision of luxury. This rooftop delivers the ultimate blend of charm and sophistication for both a big occasion and a quick supper. With tantalizing entrees like exquisite tacos, melt-in-your-mouth sirloin, and the must-try croquetas de rabo de toro, the menu is a culinary excursion. The lunch is worth every dime, with expenses ranging from €20 to €40 per dish. The drinks? Try the Tennessee Sour for a fun variation on classic flavors; they're works of art. No matter the season, the terrace is a must-see because of its heaters and shaded tables, which give comfort all year round.

The service is just as stunning as the meal and setting. Every visit is boosted by the staff's personal touch that goes above and beyond to make your experience memorable. Are you going to witness the sunset? Nothing compares to eating the specialties of Madrid while watching the sky flush, so make sure to ask for a table with a view. To secure a premium place, reservations are recommended, especially during busy months. **Fun fact:** Despite being positioned right above the crowded Plaza del Sol, Doña Luz feels like a tranquil retreat from the bustle of the city. This enables you to dine in the middle of Madrid's vivid vibrancy and is a sort of place where memories are built and sunsets are cherished.

HIDDEN GEMS AND OFF-THE-BEATEN-PATH

Off-the-beaten-path destinations and hidden jewels are like those intriguing books you find in a library; unexpected, fascinating, and usually memorable. In Madrid, these jewels may not call out for attention, but they store a richness of tales. With hidden tapas bars as well as secret gardens, exploring these areas is like finding a secret handshake into the city's soul. Have a relaxed schedule and an open mind. The magic of these places often lies in the time you take to fully appreciate them. **Fun fact:** Many of Madrid's hidden gems were once locals-only haunts, so you're not just exploring the city but stepping into its heart and history.

- **El Capricho Park**

Tucked at *P.º de la Alameda de Osuna*, El Capricho Park is like a secret garden brought to life. This beautiful location is a refuge of calm and beauty that is only available on weekends from 9 AM to 6:30 PM. With its attractive walkways, calm lakes, and secluded places that are good for a leisurely stroll, it's the ideal spot to get away from the bustle of the city. Statues emerge from the lush greenery, and the architecture's historical appeal relates stories of its aristocratic roots in the eighteenth century. There are tons of possibilities to snap breathtaking images and enjoy the calm and quiet of the surroundings, food is not allowed inside to preserve its spotless condition so keep that in mind. Extra? It appears like a private refuge as the number of visitors is strictly managed; thus, it's never crowded.

The park's architectural marvels, including its circular bullring-inspired area; no bulls here, but allusions to an era when the aristocrats relished in dramatic entertainment, will appeal to history enthusiasts and those who desire a little whimsy. The park's appeal is found in its twisting trails and unanticipated finds, so carry comfortable shoes and a water bottle. **Fun fact:** El Capricho was established as a playground for the Dukes of Osuna, and its name means "The Whim." It surely lives up to its name.

- **Parque de la Quinta de los Molinos**

On the northeastern suburbs of Madrid, the Parque de la Quinta de los Molinos is a hidden gem and a huge park that was originally a private estate but is now a public refuge, inviting people into its lush embrace every day starting from 6:30 AM. The almond trees' flowering, which transforms the landscape into a sea of pink and white blooms, is when it truly shines in the spring. A tempting reminder that nature is as good in the city is supplied by the sweet perfume of honey. Explore the park's shady walkways, soak in the serenity, and come across charming aspects like the duck pond or the relics of its past agricultural environment, such as orchards and olive groves.

This park provides a wonderful environment for a picnic or a tranquil reprieve from the bustle of the city. All year long, the Quinta de los Molinos is just as delightful. Under the shadow of its large trees, its wide green spaces are perfect for jogging, playing fetch with your pet, or reading peacefully. Also, there are well-placed water fountains, making it the ideal area for an afternoon stroll or a morning exercise. Despite being close to the center of the city, the park's layout and rustic feel are still hearken back to its days as a finca in the countryside, giving it a sensation of time travel. If you're driving, arrive early on weekends as parking could be restricted, and visit in early March to enjoy the almond trees in their height of bloom. **Fun facts:** The park was granted to the city many years ago, and runners appreciate it due to its 2-kilometer diameter. Prepare a snack, put on your shoes, and let Quinta de los Molinos become your new favorite vacation destination.

- **Great Pond of El Retiro: Estanque Grande de El Retiro**

The Great Pond (Estanque Grande de El Retiro) is a calm oasis in the midst of Madrid's El Retiro Park, ideal for relaxing and enjoying a little piece of urban beauty. This enormous, well-known pond is flanked by lush trees and the majestic Monument to Alfonso XII, giving a lovely, perfect backdrop..

Every day starting at 10 AM, guests can hire rowboats and canoes to have a leisurely paddle over the beautiful lakes. You get to float in the pond as ducks gently glide by, street musicians sing a wonderful song, and the vivid energy of the park hums around you. The park is surrounded by gorgeous fountains and shady walks, which are great for a leisurely stroll or a little reprieve from the Spanish heat. The Great Pond, the main feature of El Retiro Park, is a UNESCO World Heritage Site. The neighboring Alfonso XII Monument, with its colonnaded architecture and lofty viewpoint of the lake, is a must-see and a well-liked place for panoramic shots.

Around the pond, there are lots of comfy seats, snack shops, and musicians where you can take in the calm and bustling ambiance. Stay hydrated by utilizing the park's water fountains, and if you're going on a weekend, try to get there early to beat the crowds for boat rentals. Bring a small lunch and sit on the monument's stairs for a nice breakfast by the lake. **Fun facts:** Originally designed for royal naval training, the pond is one of Madrid's most frequented sites. The Great Pond's attractiveness and adaptability, which blend leisure and history in a wonderful manner, make it a must-see treasure in the center of the city.

- **Estación Museo Chamberí**

Visit Madrid's quaint "ghost station" turned museum, Estación Museo Chamberí located at *Plaza de Chamberí, s/n, Chamberí*, to step back in time. As a nostalgic time capsule, this station, which was closed in 1966, was first established in 1919 as a part of Madrid's inaugural metro line. You are greeted by bright ceramic tiles, old-fashioned advertisements, and an almost tangible sensation of history as you approach the original platform. The museum gives a guided tour that lasts 30 to 40 minutes and recounts wonderful anecdotes about the history of the station, its architecture, and the development of

Madrid's metro system. Keep in mind the complete tour is in Spanish, so everyone interested in history, architecture, or rare urban gems should not miss the station's attraction and visual storytelling. To skip the large crowds and obtain priority access, register your free tickets online in advance. The rare train whooshing by on the still-in-use lines adds to the station's peculiar ambiance. Modern trains racing past this century-old relic preserved in time provide a weird contrast. The experience is nevertheless delightful, even if it would be much better with bilingual explanations, especially for people who wish to practice their Spanish or simply soak in the mood of the station.

And while you're at it, since the opening video is only in Spanish, be sure to go through it for a deeper idea of the station's history. **Interesting facts:** Known as the "ghost station" owing to its decades-long neglect, Chamberí has undergone thorough repair to restore its true charm of the early 20th century. This small piece of Madrid's history is well worth your time if you prefer learning about obscure historical occurrences or uncovering unexpected jewels. Just remember to wave to the trains that are passing by; you don't get to meet individuals from a bygone age very regularly.

- **Ermita de San Antonio de la Florida**

The Ermita de San Antonio de la Florida is a quiet chapel-turned-museum buried away at *Gta. de San Antonio de la Florida,* that contains a spectacular secret: Francisco de Goya's superb frescoes, made at the height of his creative talents. A beautiful display of cherubs, nymphs, and heavenly creatures that appear to move across the domed ceilings welcomes you inside.

This piece of art by Goya, which showcases his superb brushwork and storytelling ability, is a celebration of light and life. The burial of Goya that stands quietly beneath the towering artwork and serves as a suitable final resting place for one of Spain's most known artists, contributes to the chapel's mystical aspect. The quiet ambiance is great for truly absorbing the space's workmanship and history. Photography is strictly restricted, but admittance is free, so be sure to admire every detail with your eyes. Use the strategically positioned mirrors to your advantage to catch every detail of the frescoes without straining your neck. It is calm and quiet, remote from the noisy crowd of Madrid's major attractions, and that is what makes this modest gem even more fascinating. It does involve a brief walk or bus excursion from the city center since the Ermita is somewhat of a hidden treasure that is well worth the distance.

The peaceful environment compels visitors to remain and examine the restored frescoes that stand in strong contrast to Goya's later, more gloomy paintings. **Fun fact:** the chapel is remarkable in both architecture and legacy since it is a twin construction, but only one of them has the frescoes and Goya's remains. This is a must-visit place for art and history lovers, and also for a peaceful time in the company of beauty. After that, how about having a stroll by the surrounding river or dropping by one of the terrace cafés for a bite to eat?

- **Cerro del Tío Pío**

Cerro del Tío Pío, a hillside park that gives some of the most spectacular panoramic views of Madrid, is fondly referred to as the "Seven Tits" because of its undulating slopes. This park is a genuine treasure for experiencing a blend of urban charm and natural beauty, and it's only a metro journey from the city center. The park's seven distinctive mounds that give perfect vantage points for viewing in the famed Madrid cityscape, are the source of its moniker.

It's particularly well-liked around sunset, when the city is filled with warm pink and orange tones, making it the ideal setting for a picnic or resting with a beautiful book. The park is a terrific area for a leisurely stroll, a jog, or a game of soccer with friends because it contains sports fields, bike routes, and lots of open space. With free admission and plenty of space to unwind and re-establish a connection with nature away from the bustle of the city, Cerro del Tío Pío is open twenty-four hours a day. Here, sunsets are absolutely stunning, showering the city in a golden glow that equals that of Madrid's more frequented vantage points, such as Templo de Debod. The finest aspect? Because it's a less trafficked place, you'll observe locals drinking, speaking, and enjoying the casual environment. Nothing compares to viewing a sunset while nibbling on a spread of your favorite foods, so pack a picnic blanket and some snacks to make the most of the occasion.

Fun fact: the park has considerable historical importance as it was established on the site of shanty towns that were there for many years.

Despite its outstanding care, the park is not totally wheelchair accessible, so if accessibility is a concern, make suitable accommodations.

- **Royal Tapestry Factory: Fundación Real Fábrica de Tapices**

Modern examples of Spain's outstanding textile legacy include the Royal Tapestry Factory, often known as Fundación Real Fábrica de Tapices. Established in 1720, this historic company situated at *Calle Fuenterrabía, 2, Retiro*, has been handcrafting, utilizing age-old traditions, and

109

producing exquisite tapestries, carpets, and fabrics for over three centuries. Returning in time to explore this vibrant workshop allows you to observe talented weavers make intricate designs using the same labor-intensive techniques used in the 18th century. These gifted artists not only create fresh goods but also repair old, broken ones, therefore ensuring that Spain's textile legacy lives for many more years. This is a completely working studio where history and art come to life right before your eyes, not your typical museum.

What truly distinguishes a visit is the guided tour, providing fascinating insights into the intricate weaving technique. The experience; witnessing the meticulous creation of silk and yarn and witnessing the construction of large tapestries on massive looms, is both educational and visually stunning. Don't miss the chance to see some amazing older works showing the evolution of Spanish tapestry-making. Check their schedules ahead of time, as the English tour only takes place one time per day. Also, in order to retain the exclusivity of active projects, avoid taking photographs while you're there. **Fun fact:** It was crucial in fixing tapestries destroyed during World War II, proof of the factory's continuing importance. If you're driving, be cautious of the parking limits; fines are taken quite seriously in Madrid.

- **Museo Geominero**

Ancient artifacts and exquisite architecture cohabit together at Madrid's Museo Geominero, a fascinating study of the discipline of geology tucked at *C. de Ríos Rosas, 23, Chamberí*. The museum is set in a beautiful edifice that resembles a 19th-century palace of science, replete with grand balconies and a domed glass ceiling. With a wide collection of minerals, fossils, and diamonds from all over the globe, in addition to treasures that are unique to Spain, the shows are a visual feast. It can be a peek into Spain's volcanic past or the secrets buried beneath the petrified bones of animals that stretch back millions of years, meaning every case has a narrative to tell. As spectacular as the relics stored within, the edifice itself is a marvel of art. And here's an extra; it is one of Madrid's best-kept secrets for a budget friendly vacation, as admittance is free. Part of the excitement is traversing the museum; simply find the major exhibitions on the first floor. The displays are intriguing enough to enchant any visitor, regardless of linguistic barriers, even though the signage is largely in Spanish. Get there early, as the museum closes promptly at 2:00 PM. Also, don't get caught up in the enchantment since they will turn out the lights when it's time to go.

Don't miss the informative display on the volcanic outburst in the Canary Islands and the devoted area on Spain's geological treasures. **Fun fact:** Many of the museum's spectacular specimens were provided by committed collectors and organizations worldwide, so they are not merely for exhibition. The Museo Geominero gives a very exceptional experience that marries knowledge with a hefty dose of wonder. Remember to smile during the security check; they're guarding the world's most valuable items.

- **Pantheon of Illustrious Men: Panteón de España**

A hidden gem in Madrid's Retiro area is the Pantheon of Illustrious Men, recently renamed the Pantheon of Spain. This neo-Byzantine treasure set at *C. Julián Gayarre, 3, Retiro,* was created between 1892 and 1899, and is a refuge of beauty, history, and restrained devotion. The cloister's beautiful design and the marble sculptures' superb craftsmanship are equally breathtaking. This place recognizes the historical personalities who inspired Spain's democracy and cultural growth, including politicians, soldiers, and other noteworthy individuals.

Renowned sculptors Mariano Benlliure and Agustín Querol designed the tombs, which are masterpieces of funeral art. The majestic Statue of Liberty in the courtyard that Ponciano Ponzano built in 1853 out of Carrara marble, is not to be missed. **Fun fact:** this statue is 26 years older than the well-known New York monument. It serves as a touching reminder of Spain's contributions to the concepts of justice and freedom. Despite its tiny size, its pleasant environment makes it the perfect location for both art and history fans. The narratives of individuals like Canalejas, Cánovas, and Ríos Rosas are mirrored in the mausoleums, blending grandeur and grace. As you wander, stop to observe how the cloister's mild light enhances the neo-medieval architecture and offers the place a serene, almost magical sense. Get there early to appreciate the peace and quiet before the occasional school group enlivens the halls, especially on weekends. Be cautious to time your visit around avoiding its Monday closure, while entrance is free and guided tours are given to improve your experience.

- **Real Botanical Garden Alfonso XIII: Real Jardín Botánico Alfonso XIII**

The Real Botanical Garden Alfonso XIII is a pleasant and serene oasis nestled away at *Av. Complutense, s/n, Moncloa,* in the midst of Madrid's university campus. A trip along its lush corridors is like entering a living artwork, where visitors of all ages are delighted by nature; inspired exhibitions and butterflies flutter among beautiful flower beds. This garden is accessible on weekdays from 8:30 AM to 7 PM (closed on weekends), and offers a quiet break from the bustle of the city. Seasonal flowers, properly picked plant collections, and the occasional bird sound give a tranquil mood that is great for individuals who appreciate the outdoors. Don't miss the rotating exhibitions that frequently contain magnificent nature photography or textile art; evidence of the strong relationship between creativity and the natural world.

Its versatility is what actually makes this plant refuge remarkable. The garden is turned into a colorful outdoor concert area during the summer. Imagine sipping a cool drink while sitting on the grass beneath ancient trees, all the while listening to live music in the evening. The joyful ambiance is accentuated by food trucks and artisan stalls, making it the perfect venue for a laid-back evening with friends. **Fun fact:** As you meander around this garden, listen for the cheerful sounds of the unexpectedly broad assortment of bird species that call it home. For a more leisurely experience, visit in the morning and carry a lovely book to read in one of the shaded alcoves.

- **Museo La Neomudéjar**

For those who prefer bold, avant-garde art, the Museo La Neomudéjar is a true gold mine, nestled at *C. de Antonio Nebrija*, in an antique industrial edifice that was originally a part of Madrid's Atocha train station. You can explore this grungy, intriguing venue, whose weathered walls and peeling paint offer a raw, appealing backdrop for contemporary art, for $6 (€5) per person. This gallery is an artist's utopia and a visitor's pleasure, specializing in graffiti, politically charged artwork, video art, and avant-garde installations. Bold, provocative, and sometimes even disturbing, the displays blend in nicely with the building's industrial beauty. It gives a unique midweek getaway into a creative world and is only available Wednesdays and Thursdays beginning at 11 AM. A modest garden with chairs and tables gives a tranquil space to contemplate, drink, or shoot some images for social media. La Neomudéjar's dedication to offering a platform for up-and-coming artists, including residencies and lots of area for their creative activities, is what makes it so enticing. Explore passageways filled with creepy sounds or stumble upon artworks fashioned from discarded metal. It is pretty amazing to observe how modern art and historic architecture can coexist. To obtain free entrance if you're in Madrid on a Wednesday morning, organize your visit between 11 AM and 1 PM. **Fun fact:** The museum's industrial look and historical relevance derive from its earlier service as a Renfe train workshop.

- **Jardines de San Francisco**

The Jardines de San Francisco is a calm oasis with well-kept gardens, vibrant flower beds, and breathtaking elevation perspectives that is snuggled away at *Gran Vía de San Francisco.* The historic grounds of the former Convent of San Francisco, which was demolished in the middle of the 20th century, are now home to this charming park. These days, it's a serene refuge great for a long stroll or some reflection. Particularly in May, when they blossom in a symphony of hues; yellow, pink, and red, and are tastefully labeled for your eager inquiry, the rose gardens steal the show. As you gaze at the heavenly sculptures, statues like "The Dream of San Francisco" add an artistic touch and make you wonder about the saint's dreams. And in the gardens' rear? A secluded place with broad views of the Casa de Campo, the Manzanares River, and, on a clear day, even the snow-capped mountains.

These gardens give everything you could possibly desire; can be history, the outdoors, or maybe a tranquil spot to unwind. The neighboring terraces and benches give perfect locations to relax, especially after sunset when the city is magnificently lighted by the golden light. To fully enjoy the bohemian feel, visit in late spring when the roses are in full bloom and bring a book or notebook. **Fun fact:** It is claimed that Saint Francis himself may have stayed here on his pilgrimages, and the earliest convent on this location dates back to the 12th century.

- **Editorial Mundo Negro**

Editorial Mundo Negro, nestled at *C. de Arturo Soria,* behind the Comboni Missionaries' main building in Madrid, is a true treasure mine for those interested in African art, history, and culture. The Comboni Missionaries developed this magazine in the 1960s as a method of marketing their primary publications, Mundo Negro and Aguiluchos, which enliven African stories for both children and adults.

It has evolved into a vibrant center for missionary and cultural publications over the years, with a collection of more than 140 volumes and 20 DVDs spanning everything from the historical to the spiritual. With a focus on portraying Africa's rich and diverse past, this editorial serves as a significant resource for the Church and its international mission. These cultural gems are only a click away from their online shop if you can't make it to their welcome physical location. But wait; there's more; The facility is also a comprehensive cultural experience that includes an African museum on the first floor and an African-themed library on the third. There are numerous publications here to capture your curiosity for both adult educational experience and children's fiction. Before the 2:30 PM closing time, visit on a weekday morning to properly experience the venue. Don't forget to pick up a copy of Mundo Negro, it acts as a doorway to stories that actually transport you.

Fun fact: As one of the most well-documented writings on Africa and missionary activity in Spain, this editorial is a fantastic resource for researchers, educators, and everyone interested in different cultures.

- **Museo de San Isidro**

The Museo de San Isidro, a delightful treasure that gives an informative trip through the city's history from the Paleolithic age to the present, is nestled at *Pl. de San Andrés*. Anthropology, archeology, and local folklore are all brilliantly blended in this modest but powerful museum, united by the narrative of San Isidro, Madrid's cherished patron saint. Accessible without charge, it's great for a quick and stimulating breather between exploring the busy neighborhood and savoring tapas at nearby places. With interactive touchscreens, magnificent Roman mosaics, and even the relics of elephants and mammoths, the displays are well thought out. Don't miss the well, which is claimed to be the scene of one of San Isidro's miracles, and the sculptures in the courtyard. Despite being short (about 40 minutes), the experience is noteworthy because it gives a look into the lives of Madrid's original occupants and the city's steady evolution over the decades.

The accessibility of this museum and its innovative focus on everyday people rather than elite politics or royalty. Explore its corridors to learn about the manufacture of tools, observance of burial rituals, and the evolution of the city from a modest town into the flourishing metropolis it is today. One of the highlights is a magnificent 3D map of historical Madrid that eloquently portrays the history of the city. With exhibits that examine their lives and miracles, the museum also celebrates San Isidro and his wife, Saint María de la Cabeza, who are supposed to have dwelt here. Since the museum is closed on Mondays and closes at 8 PM, arrange your visit early in the day. It's the perfect way to merge history with current Madrid, so while you're here, go to the local market for a bite to eat. **Fun fact:** For decades, the inhabitants of San Isidro have congregated to drink from the mystical water of the well on the feast day.

- **Parque Juan Carlos I: Parque de Juan Carlos I**

Parque Juan Carlos I is an urban oasis nestled at *GLORIETA S.A.R. DON JUAN DE BORBON,* on the outskirts of Madrid. This vast park has everything for a leisurely stroll, work out and a space for a nice family day. The lakes, olive orchards, and greenery are stunning and the region is also a hub of activity. Try canoeing or fishing on one of the quiet lakes, take a free train journey within the park, or hire a bike (remember to bring your ID). Children will adore the various playgrounds with their specific equipment, while art fans will be in awe of the modern sculptures strewn across the park for an unexpected artistic aspect to the surrounding environment. With its well-kept lawns, paths, and designated activity spaces, the park, constructed in 1992, is a modern masterpiece that is excellent for picnics, jogging, or resting with a good book under the trees' shade. Because the park is so extensive, you should give enough time to see all of its attractions. With fewer visitors and gentler temperatures, the park is especially tranquil in the early hours of the day and is open every day at 7 AM.

An intriguing reality is that you can be lucky enough to uncover a surprise or two, such as tortoises in some of the ponds, which will add a little natural enchantment to your vacation. And if you chance to be there around sunset, get ready to be delighted as the park is lit by a golden glow that is excellent for a calm way to close off the day.

SHOPPING AND SOUVENIRS

Shopping in Madrid is like going on a treasure hunt because of the availability of interesting boutiques. These small gems are an experience; quirky, trendy, and brimming with individuality. Madrid's boutique scene is bound to surprise you regardless of what you might be shopping for. These establishments, which feature contemporary design and vintage treasures, give a nice break from the conventional chain merchants. In addition to the prospect of discovering something genuinely unusual, you'll also receive a taste of Madrid's sense of style in adorable miniature packaging. And take your time, wander the narrow streets of neighborhoods like Malasaña or Chueca, and you'll find hidden boutiques tucked away in the most unexpected places. And hey, don't be afraid to chat with the owners; they more or less have fascinating stories to share about their pieces;

- **Malababa Serrano**

Malababa Serrano is a must-visit for anyone seeking classic products that mix current design with traditional craftsmanship. This business, situated at *C. de Serrano* area, has a handpicked range of handbags, shoes, and jewelry that emit a simple, subtle elegance. Malababa distinguishes itself for its attention to ethical production, the use of quality materials, and the rehabilitation of traditional artisanal traditions. You can say; it is a celebration of Spanish culture and ecologically responsible design, with each product offering a message of sustainability, creativity, and craftsmanship.

You can explore Malababa's offerings during the rest of the week as it is closed on Mondays. Spend some time appreciating the artistry that goes into each piece, and don't be hesitant to ask the knowledgeable staff about the materials and processes they employed. **Fun fact:** Did you know that Malababa designs and manufactures their goods locally in Spain? This guarantees that each item benefits the community and minimizes the carbon footprint of the firm. With the assurance that your purchase is both ethical and appealing, it's the perfect destination to shop guilt-free.

- **Cortana Madrid**

    Cortana Madrid is a hidden gem situated at *C. de Jorge Juan,* for those searching for classic elegance, gorgeous wedding dresses, and finely created ready-to-wear goods. The store's beautiful, tranquil environment takes you to a world where high craftsmanship and luxury coexist, and every piece of apparel appears like an artwork. The creative power behind Cortana, Rosa Esteva, has built a brand that is as much about the fabric's history as it is about its design.

    Esteva herself designed the unusual watercolor patterns that typically showcase the collections' natural, quality materials. You can sense the passion and attention to detail that goes into each item as you walk in. The boutique has a pleasant, almost secretive feeling, particularly in the bridal area, which is like a hidden paradise of lovely dresses. To thoroughly appreciate the customized attention the staff is recognized for, try to arrange your appointment in advance if you want to visit Cortana. The crew is always glad to supply advice customized to your preferences and wants. **Fun fact:** Because of Cortana's unusual design, every wedding gown is conceived and constructed with the greatest degree of precision; in fact, it's highly common for guests to find that their dress fits beautifully without the need for any alterations. Also, bear in mind that the boutique is open from 11am to 8pm (excluding Sundays), providing you ample time to completely appreciate this unique experience.

- **Antón Martín Market:** Mercado Antón Martín

Mercado Antón Martín, a colorful and real treasure that delivers a variety of cuisines, cultures, and local charm, is nestled at *C. de Sta. Isabel, 5,* near the Antón Martín metro station. In contrast to Madrid's more tourist-heavy markets, this two-story gem appears surprisingly authentic; a less crowded but quiet neighborhood where locals purchase fresh vegetables and visitors delight in foreign cuisine. Every mouthful here is an experience, like the sushi-grade fish in the Japanese restaurant Yoka Loka and fresh oysters at El Tarantín. With modern additions like specialist coffee cafes and craft beer sellers, the market is alive with the vigor of old-fashioned commerce. The aroma of sizzling tapas and fresh vegetables creates an atmosphere as much as a meal. One expert tip is to arrive early in the day when the market is less busy or arrange your meals wisely, as several establishments take breaks between lunch and dinner.

If nature calls, don't forget to ask for the bathroom code; it's a pleasant touch that ensures the facilities remain hygienic for visitors. Its modest size and tiered architecture make it seem like a snug treasure hunt. Interesting fact? The market maintains its pulse firmly in sync with the creative vitality of the city by periodically presenting public events and seminars in addition to food.

- **Mercado de la Cebada**

Mercado de la Cebada is a bustling two-story market combining classic elegance with a little modern design. It's situated at *Pl. de la Cebada,* in the old La Latina neighborhood of Madrid. Covering over 6,000 square meters, this market is a real treasure mine of artisan goods, fresh fruit, meats, and seafood. With brilliant vegetables and Iberian hams, the food is as fresh as it gets and attracts both locals and curious visitors. Mercado de la Cebada serves not only as a grocery market, but also as a hub for fashion, art, and unique businesses like a shoe repair shop and a law office that handles divorce claims. On weekends, the market turns into a busy culinary paradise as vendors create regional specialties, seafood platters, and scrumptious tapas. The arched ceilings whisper laughter, clinking cocktails, and the unique bustle of Madrileño life.

This market is special as it masterfully blends the ancient with the new. Alongside the arts and crafts stalls, charming cafés, and even a laundry, you can chat to a butcher about the right cut for your stew. To see the market at its busiest, go on a Saturday afternoon. As retailers clean out their weekend items, they occasionally offer tapas at great rates.

Furthermore, the 24-hour parking lot of the market offers discounts to consumers driving who spend more than €10 an hour. **Fun fact:** The huge open space of Mercado de la Cebada used to conduct sporting events as well as theatrical plays. It is now a real, breathing illustration of Madrid's vibrant feeling of community.

- **Mercado de San Fernando**

A hidden gem that expertly mixes regional charm with culinary adventure, Mercado de San Fernando is situated at *C. de Embajadores,* in Madrid's busy Lavapiés district. A destination for foodies and curious visitors alike, this colorful indoor market boasts a remarkable array of gourmet sellers, fresh veggies, and odd products. Authentic tapas, a cold sip of vermouth, or international street food are all wonderfully provided at this market. Locals converge in San Fernando to shop, eat, and meet up over affordably priced beers, maintaining a more laid-back vibe. The market is the ideal spot to grab a meal of tapas for €1 or a craft beer while soaking in the colorful environment as it comes alive with a pleasant bustle in the evening.

The market's informality and variety with mouthwateringly crispy empanadas as well as vegan delights and specialty liquors, are what make it so enticing. For the total experience, especially on a Friday or Saturday night, visit at 8 PM when the bars and stalls are in full action. Also, if you get there early, don't sweat about the initial hush; it's simply the lull before the gastronomic storm. **Fun fact:** This mercado is a paradise for anybody searching for more than just food, as it also includes unusual items like vinyl records, secondhand books, and homemade crafts. The inviting setting, courteous shopkeepers, and superb food more than make up for the somewhat of a key-to-toilet treasure hunt (keep an eye out for signs).

- **Mercado de Chamberí**

A charming combination of tradition and innovation, Mercado de Chamberí is nestled at *C. de Alonso Cano,* in the midst of Madrid's Chamberí area and delivers a bustling experience for both foodies and curious travelers. A feast for the eyes and the taste, this bustling market is a real gold mine of fine veggies, meats, seafood, cheeses, nuts, and preserves and the market provides a dynamic combination of contemporary cuisine and vintage charm. The neighborhood is pleasant, immaculate, and full of personality, making it another one of those cool places to spend a lot of time. Alao, the laid-back restaurants and bars here are great for resting with a drink and some supporting company for folks who appreciate a good sporting event with their tapas.

Offering traditional Spanish food as well as current gourmet creations, the market's culinary offerings are nothing short of extraordinary. With highlights like the beautifully golden truffled pecorino cachopo and the honey-type artisanal breads (try the bakery). **Pro tip:** "Cafetería - Bar Chamberí," with its welcoming atmosphere and reasonably priced tapas menu, is a great place to start your trip. Did you know that the market has been a mainstay of the neighborhood for many years and that it extends across Alonso Cano Street? Without sacrificing the friendliness and genuineness that residents love, its recent development has introduced more inventive and alternative possibilities.

SIMPLE SAMPLE ITINERARIES

A 7-day Family-Focused Itinerary: Activities for All Ages

Day 1:

- Start your trip at the Royal House of Madrid, Europe's biggest working royal house, where you can walk through opulent rooms and imagine royal life.

- After exploring this beautiful landmark, treat yourselves to a delicious tortilla de patatas at Casa Dani, a family favorite for original Spanish tastes.

- Spend your afternoon at El Retiro Park, where rowboats on the lake and the magical Crystal Palace make memories for everyone. The vast green spaces let kids burn off energy while adults soak up the beauty of the parks.

- In the evening, enjoy lively tapas sharing at Malaspina, the kind of spot where every bite feels like a party.

Fun Fact: The Crystal Palace at El Retiro Park was originally built as a nursery to house tropical plants from the Philippines. It's a gem of a 19th-century building.

Day 2:

- Make history come alive at the Museo Nacional del Prado, where a scavenger hunt for works like Las Meninas turns art into an exciting game.

- Recharge with a farm-to-table lunch at La Vaca y La Huerta, where every dish feels like a work of art itself.

- Wander through the Real Jardín Botánico in the afternoon, looking at themed gardens and bright blooms.

- End the day with a flamenco show at Las Tablas, where the passionate beats and dramatic moves capture all ages.

Fun Fact: The Museo del Prado houses over 8,600 paintings, but only about 1,500 are on show at any given time. It's like finding different secret gems each time.

Day 3:

- Head to Parque de Atracciones de Madrid for a morning of exciting rides and family-friendly activities.

- After a morning of fun, enjoy a colorful lunch at Rosi La Loca, a playful eatery bursting with color and taste.

- Spend your afternoon visiting Casa de Campo, Madrid's biggest green space, with its zoo, fishing choices, and cable car rides. The panoramic views of the city skyline from the cable car are simply stunning.

Day 4:

- Explore the charming El Capricho Park, where an enchanting maze and calm paths create a magical escape.

- For lunch, enjoy the fresh and seasonal flavors at Angelita Madrid. In the afternoon, the Museo Geominero reveals a dazzling collection of rocks and fossils that will fascinate interested minds.

- Wrap up the day with a walk to Mercado de San Fernando, where casual eats and unique local items await.

Fun Fact: El Capricho Park's maze was originally created to entertain nobles in the 18th century. Who can find their way out the fastest?

Day 5:

- Immerse yourselves in the spirit of sports at Santiago Bernabéu Stadium, home to Real Madrid. Tour the stadium, learn about its fascinating past, and snap some wonderful pictures.

- Enjoy a classy lunch at El Paraguas before going to Mercado de Chamberí. This lively market is excellent for tasting fresh fruit, shopping for handmade goods and enjoying the bright atmosphere.

Fun Fact: Santiago Bernabéu Stadium has a standing capacity of over 81,000, making it one of the biggest venues in Europe. It's a dream spot for sports fans.

Day 6:

- Take a break from the city with a day trip to San Lorenzo de El Escorial, a UNESCO World Heritage Site. Explore the beautiful monastery, grounds, and library while taking in the history and beauty of this amazing site. Pack a picnic for a relaxed family lunch amidst the beautiful settings.

Day 7:

- Spend your final day relaxing at Parque Juan Carlos I, where art gardens, bike trails, and quiet lakes offer the perfect goodbye to your Madrid trip.

- For lunch, enjoy a mix of flavors at Sacha Restaurant for its creative and comfortable food. Take a final walk through Madrid Río, thinking about the memories made, and toast to an amazing family holiday.

Bring comfortable walking shoes and a reusable water bottle to keep everyone hydrated and satisfied during your travels.

A 7-Day First-Timer's Madrid Itinerary

Day 1:

- Kick off your Madrid trip at the Royal Palace of Madrid, a jaw-dropping testament to Spanish wealth and history. Wander through its golden rooms, wonder at the Throne Room, and think what it might feel like to live here (spoiler: a lot of cleaning staff would be needed).

- Cross the square to the Catedral de la Almudena, where its modern painted glass adds a splash of unexpected color to tradition.

- For dinner, dive into a tapas crawl along Calle de la Cava Baja, where every bite is a beauty.

Fun Fact: The Royal House of Madrid has 3,418 rooms, making it the biggest royal house in Europe. Imagine trying to find your keys in there.

Day 2:

- Spend the morning getting lost in the wonders at Museo Nacional del Prado. From Velázquez to Goya, the world-class art here will make even reluctant museumgoers pause in awe.

- Grab lunch at El Paraguas for its upscale and comfortable take on Asturian food. In the afternoon, wander through El Retiro Park, stopping by the Crystal Palace to soak in some quiet magic.

- End your day at one of Madrid's hip rooftop bars, like Ginkgo Sky Bar, with views that will make you want to stay forever.

Fun Fact: El Retiro Park was once a royal playground and is home to over 15,000 trees, making it a UNESCO World Heritage Site.

Day 3:

- Start your day at Puerta del Sol, the busy heart of Madrid, where locals meet at the famous Bear and Strawberry Tree statue.

- Wander over to Plaza Mayor, taking in the history and lively street artists. For lunch, indulge in Madrid's famous calamari sandwich at Casa Revuelta; it's messy, delicious, and oh-so-Madrid.

- Spend the afternoon exploring Mercado de San Miguel, a paradise of gourmet bites and local tastes.

Fun Fact: The figure at Puerta del Sol isn't just cute; it reflects Madrid's past ties to agriculture and wildlife.

Day 4:

- Take a morning trip to San Lorenzo de El Escorial, where Spain's past unfolds in a beautiful mix of convent, castle, and library.

- Back in the city, visit the Royal Basilica of Saint Francis the Great for its breathtaking dome and calm beauty.

- Wrap up the day with a cozy dinner at Sacha Restaurant, mixing creative flair with traditional Spanish warmth.

Day 5:

- Dive into the Passion of Madrid at Santiago Bernabéu Stadium. If you're a die-hard fan or just going along for the ride, the excitement of this place is infectious.

- For lunch, savor the lively foods at Rosi La Loca, a diner as colorful as its menu.

- In the evening, immerse yourself in the fiery beats of a flamenco show at Cardamomo Tablao Flamenco; it's a classic Madrid experience that will leave you in awe.

Fun Fact: Flamenco isn't just a dance; it's a UNESCO-listed cultural treasure, based in Andalusian, Gypsy, and Moorish customs.

Day 6:

- Step into the modern art world at Museo Nacional Centro de Arte Reina Sofía, home to Picasso's famous Guernica.

- Grab a late lunch at La Vaca y La Huerta, where fresh, seasonal foods shine. Spend your afternoon at Casa de Campo, a large park with enough activities to please everyone, rowboats as well as a cable car ride.

Fun Fact: The Reina Sofía museum was previously a hospital before changing into a cultural haven. Art really does heal.

Day 7:

- Take a morning walk through Parque Juan Carlos I, a modern park filled with statues and peaceful paths.

- Stop for churros and hot chocolate at the famous Chocolatería San Ginés; it's the sweetest way to end your trip.

- Spend your afternoon picking up gifts at Mercado de San Fernando, where local artists and colorful food stalls will leave you spoiled for choice.

Pro Tip: Download a translation app before your trip; it'll help with choices, directions, and making links with locals. You'll be saying "gracias" like a pro in no time.

A 7-Day Romantic Madrid Itinerary

Day 1:

- Start your love getaway at the Royal Basilica of Saint Francis the Great, where the elaborate paintings and calm surroundings set the mood for your trip.

- Stroll over to Jardines de San Francisco, a peaceful spot for quiet times together.

- In the evening, indulge in a cozy meal at Restaurante Sacha for its private setting and gourmet delights.

Fun Fact: The dome of the Royal Basilica of Saint Francis the Great is one of the biggest in Christendom, rivaling St. Peter's Basilica in Rome.

Day 2:

- Spend your morning at the Museo del Romanticismo, an ode to 19th-century art, love, and writing.

- After taking in the romance, walk through El Capricho Park, one of Madrid's most charming and lesser-known green areas.

- End the day with drinks at La Terraza de Óscar, where the views of Madrid's city are almost as breathtaking as your partner.

Fun Fact: El Capricho Park was commissioned by a queen in the 18th century as a love retreat; perfect for couples.

Day 3:

- Explore the historic Pantheon of Illustrious Men in the morning, followed by a walk to the serene Real Jardín Botánico Alfonso XIII for a quiet escape.

- As the day fades, enjoy a flamenco show at Café Ziryab, a smaller, more private setting for experiencing Spain's passionate art form.

Fun Fact: The Real Jardín Botánico Alfonso XIII hosts a collection of rare plants from around the world, adding a touch of wonder to your visit.

Day 4:

- Take a day trip to the Royal Site of San Lorenzo de El Escorial, a gem of Spanish Renaissance building.

- Upon returning to Madrid, head to Estación Museo Chamberí, a beautifully renovated metro stop frozen in time.

- For dinner, visit Riveira do Miño and share a delicious seafood platter; because nothing says love like sharing your food.

Fun Fact: San Lorenzo de El Escorial was once the summer getaway of Spanish royalty, and its grounds remain a haven for romance.

Day 5:

- Spend your morning visiting **Parque de Juan Carlos I**, a vast and calm park ideal for long walks and quiet talks.

- Later, visit **Museo Geominero** for a unique experience browsing beautiful gems and rocks.

- In the evening, delight in fine eating at El Club Allard, where every dish is made like a work of art.

Fun Fact: Museo Geominero's dazzling collection includes fossils, rocks, and jewels from all over Spain; a true treasure trove.

Day 6:

- Visit Mercado de San Fernando for breakfast and pick up local treats.

- Stroll through Parque Madrid Río, where the riverside views and modern design make for a lovely trip.

- As the sun sets, treat yourselves to a Michelin-starred dinner at El Paraguas, where the setting and tastes are memorable.

Fun Fact: Mercado de San Fernando is not just a market; it's a lively place for locals, with live music and events on weekends.

Day 7:

- On your last day, walk through the Ermita de San Antonio de la Florida, a secret gem with beautiful paintings.

- Spend your final afternoon at Parque de la Quinta de los Molinos, where beautiful almond trees create a magical atmosphere.

- Finish with a sunset drink at Ginkgo Restaurante & Sky Bar, toasted to a trip full of love and excitement.

Pro Tip: Take your time at each location; Madrid rewards those who stay. Share a coffee or a kiss in a quiet spot, and don't rush the magic.

PRACTICAL TRAVEL TIPS

Budget Breakdowns for Madrid on the Move

Getting around Madrid doesn't have to drain your wallet; it's surprisingly affordable, quick, and even a little fun, and there's a choice for every type of tourist and budget. Let's break it down so you can move through the city like a pro (and maybe even have enough left over for an extra churro or two).

- **The Metro:**

Madrid's train system is one of the best in Europe, and it's easy on the wallet. A single ticket costs around €1.50 to €2.00, based on how many zones you cross. But if you're going to explore the city for a few days, grab a 10-trip ticket for €12.20; it's a steal and works for both the metro and city buses. Oh, and if you're coming into Madrid, the metro from the airport is just €5.00, including a small airport extra. Download the Metro de Madrid app for live updates and route planning; it's your digital lifesaver during rush hour.

Fun Fact: The Madrid metro runs over 300 kilometers and has a stop named after the TV show La Casa de Papel (Money Heist). Perfect for fans to geek out.

- **City Buses:**

If you prefer a more beautiful trip, hop on a city bus. Tickets are €1.50 per ride, but that trusty 10-trip ticket works here too. Buses are a great way to see Madrid's neighborhoods without feeling like you're stuck underground. For night owls, the "búhos" (owl buses) run after the metro shuts down, ensuring you get home safely without spending on a cab. Sit near the front for the best views; and to chat with the driver if you need tips. Madrileños are super friendly.

Fun Fact: Madrid's buses are becoming greener, with a growing number of electric and hybrid choices zipping through the city.

- **Taxis and Rideshares:**

While cabs and rideshares like Uber and Cabify are convenient, they're best left for late nights or airport trips. A normal ride across town costs around €8 to €15, while airport trips average €30 flat. If you're going as a group, sharing the fare makes this a fair choice. So opt for rideshares during busy hours to avoid cab fees.

Fun Fact: Madrid's cabs have a red stripe and a green light on top when they're free; just flag one down like a local.

Biking:

Madrid's bike-share program, BiciMAD, lets you take an electric bike for as little as €2 for the first hour. It's a wonderful way to explore parks like Madrid Río or El Retiro while enjoying the sunshine. Just beware: Madrid has hills, and they're no joke. Stick to bike lanes and quieter streets to make the most of your ride.

Fun Fact: BiciMAD bikes are provided with electric help, so you can handle those hills with ease; just think you're doing all the work.

<u>Budget Breakdown Sample (Per Day)</u>

- Metro/Bus Pass: €4 (assuming 4 rides a day)
- Occasional taxi/rideshare: €5-10 (optional)

- Bike Rental (1 hour): €2

Daily Total: Around €10-15

With these choices, you can navigate Madrid easily without blowing your budget. The city's charm lies not just in its sites but in the trip itself. So grab your map (or phone), pick your ride, and let Madrid's magic take you away.

Madrid Packing Checklist

Travel Documents
Passport (valid for at least six months)
Visa (if applicable)
Health/travel insurance documents
Flight tickets or boarding passes (physical or digital)
Hotel or Airbnb reservation details
Itinerary or list of planned activities
Copies of important documents (stored separately)
Local currency (Euros) and credit/debit cards
Contact information for emergencies (embassy, hotel, family)
Clothing
Light, breathable layers for daytime exploring
Comfortable walking shoes for cobblestone streets
Dressy outfit and shoes for evenings (Madrid

loves to dress up)

Seasonal outerwear:

- Spring/Fall: Light jacket or blazer
- Winter: Warm coat, scarf, gloves
- Summer: Hat, sunglasses, and sunscreen

Casual tops and bottoms: jeans, skirts, or shorts (weather-dependent)

Underwear, socks, and sleepwear (enough for your trip + 1 extra)

Swimwear (if you plan to visit a rooftop pool or spa)

Toiletries

Toothbrush, toothpaste

Shampoo, conditioner, body wash (travel size if needed)

Deodorant

Skincare products: Cleanser, moisturizer, sunscreen (SPF is a must)

Hairbrush/comb

Makeup and shaving kit (if applicable)

Feminine hygiene products

Any prescription medications

Electronics

Smartphone and charger

Universal power adapter (Spain uses Type F plugs and 230V voltage)

Power bank

Camera and accessories (optional but recommended for photographers)

Headphones/earbuds

E-reader or tablet for travel entertainment

Miscellaneous Must-Haves

Reusable water bottle (many fountains offer drinkable water)

Small umbrella or raincoat (Madrid weather can be unpredictable)

Reusable shopping bag (eco-friendly and handy for markets)

Travel pillow for long flights or train rides

Lightweight daypack for carrying essentials

Ziploc bags for liquids or snacks

> First-aid kit: Band-aids, painkillers, antiseptic wipes.

- Leave room in your suitcase for Madrid's irresistible souvenirs.
- Summers can be hot; winters, chilly. Always check weather forecasts before packing.
- Madrid's restaurants are chic. A polished outfit will help you blend in with the locals.
- Dinner starts late, and nightlife kicks off even later. Comfortable and stylish outfits are key.

Madrid has more sunny days than almost any other European capital, so pack your sunnies. Tapas culture means hopping from bar to bar. A crossbody bag keeps your hands free for snacks and sangria.

Safety Tips and Local Etiquette

Madrid is a busy and friendly city, but like anywhere, learning a bit about safety and local norms will make your trip more enjoyable. You'll find the locals eager to help, more so if you show respect for their customs and follow a few simple rules;

Madrid is generally safe, but pickpocketing can happen, especially in busy places like Puerta del Sol or on public transport. Keep your goods close and use a money belt or shoulder bag. It's the old 'keep your eyes on your stuff' rule.

While Madrid's train system is wonderful, cabs are another perfect choice. Avoid calling one off the street late at night and use a trusted app like Cabify or Uber for peace of mind, especially if you're going alone or in a new area.

The metro and buses are safe and affordable, but be careful with bags and wallets. Stand close to the station edge but not too close (you never know when a crowd will rush by).

Just in case, keep the Spanish emergency number handy: 112 is for all situations, whether you need medical help or the cops.

Spaniards are big on politeness. When receiving someone, a handshake is usual, but when you're meeting people you know (or if you want to seem extra nice), a cheek kiss on both sides is the rule. Don't worry; it's not as serious as it sounds. If you're uncomfortable, a simple "Hola" and a smile work just fine.

Spaniards work hard, but they also play hard; and rest hard. Most places will close for a couple of hours in the afternoon for a nap. This is the time to rest, grab a bite, or enjoy a drink. Don't plan on shopping or hitting tourist spots between 2-5 p.m. You'll likely find yourself knocking on locked doors.

Spaniards take pride in their looks, so you'll likely see well-dressed locals wherever you go. No need for a suit, but avoid looking like you've just come from the beach or gym. When eating out, especially for dinner, dress up a little; it's a stylish way to show you're ready to accept the local vibe.

Madrid loves a long, relaxed meal, especially dinner. Don't be surprised if your dinner stretches into a two-hour event. Spaniards eat late (usually after 9 p.m.) and take their time, enjoying the tastes. You're not in a rush, so take your time.

Tapas are a big part of Madrid's society. When you order a drink, it's usual to be given a free tapa (snack), but not all bars do this; so don't expect one with every drink. Also, don't rush through tapas; they're meant to be eaten slowly, with talk and a glass of wine.

Spaniards can be a bit more touchy-feely than other countries. In a crowd, people will brush against you; it's normal. But don't push it, giving people their personal space is still important in more serious situations.

In Madrid, "¡Vale!" (pronounced: vah-leh) is the most popular word you'll hear; it's like saying "okay" or "alright." It's used to agree with something or as a general recognition. So, when in question, throw out a friendly "¡Vale!" and you'll fit right in.

Spaniards love their coffee, it's not uncommon to have a café con leche (coffee with milk) for breakfast, then another espresso after lunch. Don't be surprised if you're given coffee at almost every stop.

If you're in Madrid on a Sunday, you can't miss El Rastro; the biggest street market in Spain. It's an event where you can find odd antiques, old books, and unique gifts.

Remember, Madrid is a friendly city, and locals enjoy when tourists respect their customs. If you follow these simple tips and keep an open heart, you'll have an amazing time, taking in all the beauty, history, and energy of this incredible place.

Basic Spanish Phrases

When you're going to Madrid, you can soak in the art at the Prado or have some tapas (don't skip the patatas bravas), but also, speaking a little Spanish will definitely earn you some street respect. Don't worry, you don't need to be fluent; just a few words and phrases can go a long way in making you feel like part of the local vibe;

- **Hola (oh-lah) - Hello**

This is your magic key to the chat. It's like shaking a wand and saying, "I'm friendly, I promise!" You'll get a lot of smiles when you meet someone with a warm hola. Bonus points if you throw in a friendly "¡Qué tal!" (How's it going?) after. Locals love a lively chat.

- **Gracias (grah-see-as): thank you.**

When someone hands you a delicious croissant or holds the door for you (or even when you accidentally bump into someone on the street; oops), a quick thanks is always appreciated. It's a worldwide sign of respect, and believe me, you'll hear it a lot.

- **Por favor (por fah-vor) - please**

Use this when asking for a table at a restaurant, directions, or if you're simply being nice. Add it to any request, and suddenly you're not just a tourist; you're someone who gets the Spanish way of life.

- **¿Cuánto cuesta? (kwan-toh kwes-tah?) - How much does it cost?**

When you find that perfect gift or want to grab an espresso, this phrase is important. The seller will know you're serious about buying, and you can prepare for the number they throw your way.

- **¿Dónde está...? (dónde está?) - Where is...?**

Lost? Don't worry; it happens to the best of us. Use this one to ask for directions. For example, "¿Dónde está el Museo del Prado?" (Where is the Prado Museum?). It's your ticket to exploring the city like a pro. And if they answer in swift Spanish, just smile and nod, because you're already winning at life (you can make up by using a translation app quickly after).

- **Una cerveza, por favor (oo-nah ser-veh-thah, por fah-vor)—a beer, please.**

Madrid is famous for its local drinks (cañas), and you're going to need to try at least one. This line is your golden ticket to joining the locals at any bar. If you want to mix it up a bit, "Una copa de vino" (A glass of wine) will work wonders too.

- **Perdón, ¿hablas inglés? (per-dohn, ah-blahs een-glays?) - Excuse me, do you speak English?**

Not everyone speaks English clearly, but you'll get by. Just ask this when you're in a pinch, and you'll find that most people will be more than happy to switch to English (but don't overdo it; locals appreciate it when you try their language first).

Pro Tip: Don't stress if you don't have perfect speech. Spanish people are super understanding when it comes to non-native accents. Try to be bold and go for it, besides, they'll respect the effort. A big gracias always gets you extra points.

Fun Fact: In Madrid, people don't usually say goodbye like "goodbye" (which sounds too final), but they'll throw a "Hasta luego!" (See you later) or a joyful "Nos vemos!" (We'll see each other). Madrid is all about hope.

A Little Extra Spice for Your Vocabulary

"¿Qué tal?" (How's it going?) – Used as a welcome, but also a great way to show you're keeping the talk light and fun.

"¿Puedo ayudar?" (Can I help?) – Use it when you're feeling like a good Samaritan or when you need some quick assistance while shopping.

"Lo siento" (I'm sorry)—If you bump into someone, spill your drink, or just want to apologize for anything, this one is your magic trick.

Now, you're ready to explore Madrid, food in one hand, camera in the other, and gracias at the ready. Wherever you go in Madrid, these little lines will help you soak in all the charm and make some wonderful memories. ¡Disfruta tu viaje! (Enjoy your trip!)

Emergency Contacts and Information

It's always beneficial to have a little peace of mind when touring. I know, I know, you're all set for sightseeing, tapas, and late-night strolls around Plaza Mayor, but it's also smart to know who to call when things take an unexpected turn. Lucky for you, Madrid's got your back, and follow that, here's the important emergency info you'll want to have at the ready.

- **Emergency Number: 112**

If you need help, dial 112. It's the emergency number across Spain (kind of like 911 in the States, but cooler because it's so widely used). It covers all situations; medical problems, fire, or if you're just lost and need some help from the nice folks at the Spanish police or rescue teams. The best part? Operators can speak English, so no stress if you don't speak excellent Spanish. Just remember to breathe, and help will be on the way.

Pro Tip: Keep the number saved in your phone. Just in case, you never want to be searching for it.

The faster you call, the faster someone will help. Simple, right?

- **Police and Emergency Medical Contacts**

Sometimes, you might find yourself needing a police officer or an ambulance in a hurry. For those cases, here's what you need: Call 091 for local police incidents. They're the go-to for any law enforcement needs.

Call 061 for any medical problems. But don't worry; the great Spanish healthcare system is fast and friendly, so if you find yourself under the weather, you'll be in good hands. Madrid is home to some top-notch hospitals, so if something happens that needs professional care, you'll be in safe hands. There are plenty of hospitals across the city, but here are a couple of excellent options:

Hospital Universitario La Paz: One of Madrid's most well-known hospitals, offering great emergency care. It's well-equipped and often used by visitors.

Hospital Clínico San Carlos: Another safe choice if you're near Moncloa or need high-quality care in the city center.

For small problems, like a headache after too much sangría (we've all been there), Madrid overflows with farmacias (pharmacies) open 24/7. So if you're feeling a little off after indulging in too much jamón or just need some over-the-counter meds, check out a drugstore nearby. Many shops will have English-speaking staff.

- **Fire Department**

If the worst happens and there's a fire (fingers crossed it doesn't), you can reach the fire service by calling 080. You won't need this on your trip (we hope), but it's worth remembering.

Fun Fact: In Madrid, firemen are pretty much considered heroes. They've saved so many houses (like the famous ones around Gran Vía) and have a strong presence in the city. So, if you're near a firehouse, it's likely you'll see them grabbing a coffee or talking with locals between shifts.

- **Lost or stolen passports**

Losing your passport is never fun, but don't worry. It happens to the best of us, and there's a way to fix it. If you're from the UK, US, or another country, there's a consulate here to help you out. You'll want to call your closest office for passport problems or help.

- US Embassy: +34 917 146 300
- UK Embassy: +34 917 146 300

Pro Tip: If you can, make a print or take a picture of your passport and keep it on your phone. That way, you'll have a backup just in case. It's a small effort, but it could save you a lot of stress afterward.

When it comes to safety, there's no shame in calling for help. If you're confused or need help, don't hesitate to reach out. Madrid is a friendly city, and you'll find its people eager to lend a hand.

With this emergency info tucked into your back pocket (figuratively speaking; don't actually put it in your back pocket; it's a terrible idea), you can now enjoy your trips around Madrid and you'll be ready for anything life throws at you. Madrid may be full of surprises, but you're fully ready to meet them head-on.

Essential Touring Apps and Resources

Let's face it, exploring a lively city like Madrid can feel a bit stressful, especially when you're trying to cram the Royal Palace, El Retiro Park, and a tapas crawl into one wonderful day. But don't worry; we live in the golden age of apps, your smartphone is basically a personal tour guide, translator, and foodie expert all rolled into one. Here's a list of must-have apps and tools to make your Madrid trip as smooth as that morning café con leche.

- **Citymapper**

This app is like having a local Madrileño in your pocket. Wherever you want to go, Citymapper shows you the fastest and easiest ways. It even tells you which Metro train to take for the closest exit (mind blown, right?). The Madrid Metro is your best friend; clean, efficient, and budget-friendly. Use Citymapper to discover every part of the city without breaking a sweat.

Fun Fact: Madrid's Metro is one of the longest in the world, second only to London's Underground in

Europe. So yeah, this app will save you a lot of walking around randomly.

- **Google Translate**

Yes, Spanish is a beautiful language, but if your "Hola" and "Gracias" only get you so far, Google Translate is a lifesaver. Use it to read products, signs, or even have a quick chat with locals. The camera translation feature? Pure magic when interpreting a handwritten plate of snacks. **Pro Tip:** Download the Spanish training pack offline before your trip. That way, even if you're in a Wi-Fi dead zone (or reducing data), you can still explore the local lingo.

Fun Fact: Madrileños love their unique slang, so don't be surprised if you hear words like "¡Qué guay!" (How cool!). Google Translate might not catch the words exactly, but you'll get the idea.

- **Madrid Metro TTP**

For all things public transport, this government app is a gem. You can check Metro timetables, figure fares, and even find stops near you. If you're going to use the Metro a lot, think about getting a tourist travel pass (abono turístico) for endless rides. **Pro Tip:** The Metro is your ticket to reaching secret gems like El Capricho Park or the Temple of Debod. This app ensures you're never left stuck.

- **ElTenedor (The Fork)**

Madrid is a food lover's dream, and ElTenedor is the key to opening it. Think of it as OpenTable, but with a Spanish twist. Book tables at local places, score deals, and find hidden gems away from tourist traps. **Pro Tip:** Madrid's dinner hours are late by most standards; locals rarely eat before 9 PM. Use ElTenedor to snag a spot and accept the Spanish routine.

Fun Fact: Some of Madrid's best tapas places are standing-room-only, so don't hesitate to rub arms with locals; it's all part of the experience.

- **GuruWalk**

If you want to explore Madrid through the eyes of a local, GuruWalk offers free walking tours led by passionate locals who know the city's secrets. You can choose themes like history, street art, or even scary ghost stories. **Pro Tip:** While the walks are officially free, tipping your guide is welcomed. A few euros go a long way to show your thanks for their thoughts.

Fun Fact: Many of these guides will take you off the usual path to places like Estación Museo Chamberí or the lively Malasaña neighborhood.

- **Izi.TRAVEL**

This app makes your smartphone into a recorded tour guide. Plug in your headphones and listen to fascinating stories about Madrid's buildings, museums, and neighborhoods as you walk around. Perfect for solo tourists or anyone who loves exploring at their own pace.

Pro Tip: Download tours ahead of time to save on data. Pair this app with a relaxed walk through El Retiro Park or the Royal Botanical Garden for a wonderful afternoon.

- **Madrid Móvil**

The official app by the Madrid city council is packed with useful features, including maps, parking info, and information on city events. It's like a digital Swiss Army knife for all things Madrid.

Pro Tip: Check the events area to find free music, street markets, and cultural happenings during your stay. Madrid is always buzzing with activity; you just need to know where to look.

- **XE Currency Converter**

For foreign visitors, this app is a must. Keep track of your spending and ensure you're getting a favorable deal when swapping money. It's particularly handy when you're browsing markets like El Rastro or picking up gifts.

Pro Tip: Most places in Madrid accept cards, but having a little cash on hand for small purchases or tipping is always a beneficial idea.

- **Eventbrite or Fever**

Madrid is filled with events like dancing shows and rooftop movie nights. These apps help you find and book unique events you won't find in guidebooks (pains me to say so).

Fun Fact: Many rooftop bars, like Ginkgo Restaurante & Sky Bar, host special nights with live music. Use Fever to snag tickets and make your evenings memorable.

Armed with these apps, you'll be navigating Madrid like a seasoned tourist in no time. All in all, your smartphone will be your ideal trip partner (second only to a sturdy pair of walking shoes). Remember, Madrid is a city that rewards curiosity, so accept the adventure, apps in hand, and dive into all the magic it has to offer. ¡Buen viaje! (Have a wonderful trip!)

FINAL WORDS

As your time in Madrid draws to a conclusion, pause, contemplate, and enjoy the memories you've formed in this city of stark contrasts. Every plaza in Madrid looks to be asking you to remain a little bit longer, where sumptuous palaces and pleasant tapas cafés coexist and where history resonates through ancient cobblestones. Madrid has something to offer everyone, so perhaps you'll remember the scent of rich chocolate-covered crispy churros, the sound of street performers playing flamenco guitars, or the way the Royal Palace was lighted by the golden light of the sunset. Madrid will always be remembered because of these moments, no matter how big or minor.

Madrid is a charming city; but it's also a feeling. The streets are crowded with laughter and chatting around ten o'clock in the night. It's how locals take their time, relishing meals, sipping coffee, and living in the present. Plus, you sense yourself slowing down and harmonizing with the pulse of this charmed environment. Here's one last Pro Tip: Do something entirely unplanned before you leave.

Explore a new region, stop by a modest shop, or simply relax at a café and watch the inhabitants. The greatest unforgettable events can occasionally be uncovered by coincidence.

Fun Fact: Were you aware that Madrileños are referred to as gatos, or cats? A medieval myth about a soldier who scaled the city walls with cat-like agility is the genesis of the nickname. Whether correct or not, it's a fantastic moniker for a city that's agile and insatiably curious.

As you prepare to depart Madrid, bear in mind that this is a "see you later" rather than a "goodbye." Like the numerous travelers who have fallen in love with Madrid's charm, you will always carry a bit of Madrid with you, no matter where life takes you. Madrid has a way of luring people back. Safe travels until we meet paths again, and may you continue to smile for years to come from your memories of Madrid.

Made in the USA
Middletown, DE
25 March 2025